To Ian
Good Luck
Warren Goldfein

Diamond Gems In Autumn

50 Memorable Classics From Baseball's Golden Age, 1946-1993 From Slaughter's Run Home to Carter's Home Run

by
Warren Goldfein

Bloomington, IN  Milton Keynes, UK

AuthorHouse™
1663 Liberty Drive, Suite 200
Bloomington, IN 47403
www.authorhouse.com
Phone: 1-800-839-8640

AuthorHouse™ UK Ltd.
500 Avebury Boulevard
Central Milton Keynes, MK9 2BE
www.authorhouse.co.uk
Phone: 08001974150

© *2007 Warren Goldfein. All rights reserved.*

No part of this book may be reproduced, stored in a retrieval system, or transmitted by any means without the written permission of the author.

First published by AuthorHouse 6/22/2007

ISBN: 978-1-4259-3639-6 (sc)

Printed in the United States of America
Bloomington, Indiana

This book is printed on acid-free paper.

MANY THANKS

To my dear wife, Blossom, who did much of the legwork to help me put this project together, and put up with my erratic moods.

To my granddaughter, Erica Krouse, and family friends, Sandra Scheffer and Dorothy Grossman, who helped me to master the computer, no easy task.

To the West Orange, NJ Public Library for their excellent facilities and courteous assistance in locating reference material.

To the UPS Store, Livingston, NJ for their fine help in making bulk copies of my manuscripts.

To the memory of Joe DiMaggio and Jackie Robinson. It was from watching these two great sports legends that I first developed my love for the game of baseball.

To the Boston Red Sox. It takes a miracle for a first-time author to publish, and since the Red Sox actually managed to win a World Series, I regained the confidence it would take to find my own miracle.

AN ODE TO SHAKESPEARE

In 1994 the greedy Major League players and Club Owners failed to come to an agreement on a new contract and walked out on the fans, almost ruining the game of baseball. Two world wars, the Great Depression, and even a major earthquake could not stop baseball from holding the World Series. Only the insatiable greed of the players and owners could cancel the signature event of the national pastime.

I could not put into words my feelings for these rapacious individuals, but William Shakespeare, whom we all know was way ahead of his time, expressed it far better than I possibly could. The sports writers should award him a special place in the Baseball Hall of Fame, if only for these remarks:

"A plague o' both your houses!"

Romeo and Juliet

"The pound of flesh which I demand—is dearly bought, tis mine and I will have it. If you deny me, fie upon your law!"

The Merchant of Venice

TO THE READER

When I was growing up in Northern New Jersey, I loved playing and watching all sports, but baseball was always my favorite. With three clubs in New York, the Yankees, Dodgers, and Giants, I followed these teams and the pennant races in which they were almost always involved very closely.

In the late Forties and early Fifties, Professional Football and Basketball did not yet have the impact and national popularity they do now. They were only diversions to keep the sports-minded occupied during the Fall and Winter months, until the first pitch was thrown on Opening Day.

To me the Golden Age of baseball dawned after the end of World War Two. By the year 1946 all the great players had returned from the war fronts in Europe and the Pacific to rejoin their respective teams.

Then, when Jackie Robinson broke the Color barrier in 1947, he opened up a new channel, paving the way for all gifted athletes, whether they be Black, White, Hispanic, or Asian- anyone with the talent to compete in the major leagues, to do just that. When Robinson and those who followed entered the majors, they changed a good game into a great one.

Although I was elated to see my two hometown teams, the Yankees and Mets, finally get to meet in the World Series in 2000, I remember the days when a Subway Series was almost an annual event. October games between the Yankees and the Brooklyn Dodgers, and, in one case, a first-place National League playoff between the Dodgers and New York Giants, produced some of the most epic baseball fans have ever seen.

Over all my years of following the Diamond Sport, I suddenly realized that each year of the Golden Age seemed to produce at least one memorable game, one that had more of an impact on a pennant race, playoff, or World Series, than any other game of that season. Each one featured drama, such as Bobby Thomson's pennant-winning home run, Don Larsen's perfect game, and Willie Mays' sensational game-saving catch. Some of the contests, like the game with the wild pitch that won a pennant for the Reds, or the Series game in which the Dodgers tied a

World Series record by committing six errors, while not artistic, were still memorable classics.

I thought it would be a great idea if I could chronicle fifty of the greatest games from each year between 1946 and 1995 and provide a light, easy-to-read account of each encounter. I am reminded of some of the sports writers in early tabloid newspapers, such as Dick Young of the New York Daily News. I remember waiting for the midnight edition of the papers, so I could be the first to read about the day's ball games and get a good laugh at the clever and humorous way in which they reported the games. To me sports is entertainment and need not be taken as seriously as the hard news we read about each day, much of which is depressing and tragic.

To give each game a time frame, I have listed some of the most significant news headlines of each year. I have also noted the major sports winners of that year and the winners of the four major motion picture categories of the Academy Awards. (Trivia buffs should have fun with these results.)

Each game has a recap summary, and I have listed the heroes and goats of that game. I am reviving a practice that my early predecessors started in the tabloids.

My dilemma started when I began to realize that some years may have had more than one game that stood out from the others. For example, each of the Mets' four victories in the 1969 World Series was a classic. The 1986 postseason produced three of the most incredible contests in major league history; what to do?

In the case of the '69 Series, the fifth and final game created the moment of the Miracle Mets' triumphant victory that can never be forgotten. That game became the obvious selection.

The decision for my 1986 contest was simpler. When the club owners, players, their negotiators, and an unavailing acting commissioner (since elevated to unavailing permanent commissioner) blew off the exciting 1994 season, and with it the first World Series in ninety years because these clueless buffoons could not decide how to divide up their megamillions, I resolved that I would not chronicle any more games after the 1993 season. Thus for me the Golden Age of Baseball began with Enos Slaughter's run home and ended with Joe Carter's home run.

Since I wanted to retain an account of fifty games, I was able to incorporate each of those phenomenal '86 contests, a Red-Sox-Angels

American League playoff, a Mets-Astros National League playoff, and of course the game that fans will remember everywhere, especially in Boston, the sixth game of the World Series.

To sum up, I now offer a tableau of some of the greatest and most memorable moments in sports history in one package. I hope you enjoy reading this book as much as I enjoyed researching and writing it.

Warren Goldfein
West Orange, NJ.
August, 2006

CONTENTS

CHAPTER I: SLAUGHTER ON THE BASEPATHS 2
CHAPTER II: BEVENS MEETS THE COOKIE MONSTER ... 7
CHAPTER III A MOST UNHAPPY FELLER 11
CHAPTER IV RED SOX FAIL TO TURN THE PAGE 15
CHAPTER V ASHBURN SAVES THE DAY 21
CHAPTER VI A GIANT MIRACLE 27
CHAPTER VII IT'S UP IN THE AIR 33
CHAPTER VIII THE DRIVE FOR FIVE 38
CHAPTER IX AN A-MAYS-ING CATCH 43
CHAPTER X GLEE SHOWS IN BROOKLYN 48
CHAPTER XI A PERFECT EFFORT 53
CHAPTER XII A POLISHED ACT 59
CHAPTER XIII BRAVE HEART, TIRED ARM 65
CHAPTER XIV A TASTE OF SHERRY 71
CHAPTER XV MAZ, TERRY, AND THE PIRATES 77
CHAPTER XVI THE RAJ AND THE BABE 83
CHAPTER XVII TERRY'S REVENGE 89
CHAPTER XVIII LOOKING FOR
    BROOMS IN ALL THE RIGHT PLACES 95
CHAPTER XIX A BATTERY ASSAULT 101
CHAPTER XX SANDY'S A DANDY 107
CHAPTER XXI CATCH 22, DROP A FEW 113
CHAPTER XXII WEEKEND AT YASTRZEMSKI'S 119
CHAPTER XXIII TURNING IT AROUND 125

CHAPTER XXIV THE MOON
　　AND THE MIRACLE METS 131

CHAPTER XXV REVENGE OF THE BIRDS 137

CHAPTER XXVI THE SERIES GOES PRIME-TIME 143

CHAPTER XXVII A WILD MOOSE.. 149

CHAPTER XXVIII CAN YOU BELIEVE IT? 155

CHAPTER XXIX ONE-HIT WONDERS 161

CHAPTER XXX STAY FAIR, STAY FAIR 167

CHAPTER XXXI CHAMBLIS' GREAT ADVENTURE 173

CHAPTER XXXII REGGIE OCTOBER 179

CHAPTER XXXIII BUCKY DENTS THE SCREEN 185

CHAPTER XXXIV ONE FOR THE FAMILY 191

CHAPTER XXXV NEW FACES OF 1980 197

CHAPTER XXXVI BLUE MONDAY IN MONTREAL 203

CHAPTER XXXVII A POTENT BREW 209

CHAPTER XXXVIII DARN THOSE WHITE SOX................. 215

CHAPTER XXXIX FLUBS OF THE CUBS 221

CHAPTER XL OUT OF THE PARK WITH CLARK............... 227

CHAPTER XLI ANGELS WITH EGG ON THEIR FACES ..233

CHAPTER XLII METS HARD AS NAILS................................. 236

CHAPTER XLIII HOLD THE CHAMPAGNE—
　　IT'S THE RED SOX.. 240

CHAPTER XLIV VIOLA FIDDLES WITH CARDS 247

CHAPTER XLV "I DON'T BELIEVE WHAT I JUST SAW" .253

CHAPTER XLVI WILL THE THRILL
     AND AMAZING GRACE 259

CHAPTER XLVII A SAD NIGHT
     FOR ATHLETIC SUPPORTERS 265

CHAPTER XLVIII BRAVES'
     BAD BASERUNNING BLUNDER 271

CHAPTER XLIX FRANCISCO WHO? 277

CHAPTER L MIGHTY JOE CARTER 283

1946

MAJOR HEADLINES

Nuremberg War Tribunal convicts twenty-two German leaders of War Crimes and atrocities against humanity.

Four thousand mine workers go on strike in the U.S.

The Philippine Islands are given their independence by the United States.

SPORTS

Baseball- St. Louis Cardinals defeat Boston Red Sox in seven games.

Pro Football-Chicago Bears defeat New York Giants in the NFL final.

College Football- Notre Dame is voted National Champion.

College Basketball- Oklahoma defeats North Carolina in the NCAA final.

Hockey- Montreal defeats Boston in the Stanley Cup finals.

U.S. Open Tennis-
    Men's Finals: Jack Kramer defeats Thomas Brown Jr.
    Women's finals: Pauline Betz defeats Doris Hart.

MOVIES- ACADEMY AWARDS

Best Actor: Fredric March, *The Best Years of Our Lives*
Best Actress: Olivia de Havilland, *To Each His Own*
Best Director: William Wyler, *The Best Years of Our Lives*
Best Picture: *The Best Years of our Lives*

CHAPTER I:
SLAUGHTER ON THE BASEPATHS

Tuesday, October 15, 1946- Sportsman's Park, St. Louis, MO
World Series Game Seven, St. Louis Cardinals 4, Boston Red Sox 3

On the surface, the 1946 World Series appeared to be a huge mismatch. Led by arguably the greatest hitter of all-time, Ted Williams, and twenty-five game winning pitcher, Dave Ferris, the American League Champion Boston Red Sox roared through the regular season like a runaway freight train. The Sox won their first pennant in twenty-eight years by a margin of twelve games over the second-place Tigers.

In contrast, the National League winners, the St. Louis Cardinals, struggled through a grueling pennant race with the Brooklyn Dodgers. The two clubs ended the season tied for first place, forcing the first playoff in major league history. The Cards advanced to the Series by sweeping the Dodgers in a two-out-of –three-game showdown.

At the end of six hard-fought contests, the World Series was even, with each team having won three. The adversaries would play a seventh and deciding game on the Cardinals' home field, Sportsman's Park in St. Louis.

Fans would long remember this sudden-death struggle for its drama and tension, and for the hustling Cardinal outfielder, Enos "Country" Slaughter, scoring the winning run from first base on a routine hit to the outfield.

With each club having scored a run, the Cards broke through for a pair in the fifth inning. Murray Dickson, their good-hitting pitcher, stroked an RBI double and later scored on a single.

The Red Sox retaliated to deadlock the count in the visitors' eighth, knocking Dickson out of the game. Their outstanding center-fielder, Dom DiMaggio, doubled off the right field wall with the bases loaded to drive in the tying runs.

Cardinal manager Eddie Dyer beckoned reliever Harry Brecheen from the bullpen. The St. Louis lefty had saved the Red Birds from elimination by tossing a 4 to 1 complete-game victory two days earlier in Game Six. The tireless Brecheen then proceeded to shut down the Bosox without any further scoring in the inning.

Slaughter led off the home eighth with a single to center. Then, with two Cardinals retired, Harry Walker lined another hit to left-center. With two out, everyone in the park expected Slaughter to reach third easily. No one expected him to even attempt to score. To everyone's amazement though, that's just what he did.

Old Country just kept on going like the Energizer Bunny. As he motored around third base, the astonished shortstop, Johnny Pesky, juggled the outfield relay, holding the ball long enough for Slaughter to slide safely across the plate.

The capacity crowd roared with approval. Their heroes now stood three outs from becoming World Champions.

Boston refused to concede defeat and valiantly attempted to stay alive in the ninth. Singles by Ruddy York and Bobby Doerr put runners at the corners with only one out. Harry Brecheen then justified his unexpected appearance by retiring the next two batters on a pop up and a ground out.

While Country Slaughter scored the winning run of the Series, Brecheen displayed one of the top pitching performances in World Series history. His three victories made him the star of the October Classic.

Baseball historians rarely see the kind of double-duty heroics in a World Series, starting then relieving the next day, that Harry Brecheen showed. This kind of pitching gallantry seldom shows up unless the name in the box score is someone like Grover Cleveland Alexander or Randy Johnson.

The St. Louis Cardinals had upset the heavily-favored Boston Red Sox in an exciting World Series. The Red Birds gained a 4 to 3 victory in the tension-filled seventh game.

Enos Slaughter was the Pete Rose of his day. The hustling outfielder would never walk to a base he could run to. Sports fans will long remember Slaughter's electrifying run home as one of the most memorable moments in baseball history.

CARDINALS-RED SOX RECAP

	R	H	E
St. Louis	4	9	1
Boston	3	8	0

Winning pitcher- Brecheen
Losing pitcher- Klinger
Home Runs- none

HEROES *** Brecheen, Slaughter
GOAT < Pesky

1947

MAJOR HEADLINES

President Truman vetoes the Taft-Hartley Act, which would curb labor strikes. Congress overrides the veto.

A proposal to extend massive aid to war-torn countries in Europe is introduced by Secretary of State George C. Marshall. The proposal becomes known as the Marshall Plan.

The Truman Doctrine is enacted, when President Truman asks Congress to help Greece and Turkey stop the spread of Communist terrorism in those countries.

Jackie Robinson becomes the first black baseball player to play on a major league team, when he opens the season in the starting lineup of the Brooklyn Dodgers.

SPORTS

Baseball: New York Yankees defeat the Brooklyn Dodgers in seven-game World Series.

Pro Football: Chicago Cardinals over Philadelphia Eagles in the NFL title game.

College Football: Notre Dame is voted National Champion for the second straight year.

Pro Basketball: Philadelphia Warriors beat Chicago Stags in the first professional Championship.

College Basketball: Holy Cross defeats Oklahoma State in the NCAA finals.

Hockey: Toronto defeats Montreal to win the Stanley Cup.

U.S. Open Tennis-
    Men's finals: Jack Kramer defeats Frank Parker.
    Women's finals: Louise Brough defeats Margaret Osborne.

MOVIES- ACADEMY AWARDS

Best Actor: Ronald Coleman, *A Double Life*
Best Actress: Loretta Young, *The Farmer's Daughter*
Best Director: Elia Kazan, *Gentlemen's Agreement*
Best Picture: *Gentlemen's Agreement*

CHAPTER II:
BEVENS MEETS THE COOKIE MONSTER

Friday, October 3, 1947, Ebbets Field, Brooklyn, NY
World Series Game Four- Brooklyn Dodgers 3, New York Yankees 2

Yankee pitcher Bill Bevens was one out away from making World Series history in this fourth game of the 1947 World Series at Brooklyn's cozy little Ebbets Field. No pitcher had ever hurled a no-hitter in a World Series, but Bevens was doing just that for eight and two-thirds innings. In as bizarre an ending as any baseball game ever exhibited, he lost not only the no-hitter, but the game as well, on his final pitch.

With New York clinging to a 2 to 1 lead and two out in the ninth inning, Cookie Lavagetto belted a double off the right field scoreboard for the Dodgers' only hit. The two runners, who had both walked, scored the tying and winning runs, as Brooklyn evened the Series with a 3 to 2 victory.

Although Bevens gave up only the one hit, he walked ten, and his lack of control led to his downfall. The Dodgers scored a run without a hit in the fifth frame on two walks, a sacrifice, and an infield out.

The Yankees had scored their first run in the opening stanza, as the Yankee Clipper, Joe DiMaggio, walked with the bases loaded. The Bombers doubled their advantage in the fourth on Billy Johnson's triple and Johnny Lindell's double.

The pending climax loomed as the game entered the home ninth. With one out, Carl Furillo drew the ninth pass from Bevens. Johnny Jorgenson fouled out for the second out, leaving the anxious right-hander just one out from baseball immortality.

It was at that point that both sides displayed some most bizarre strategy as they struggled toward the finish line. Al Gionfriddo went in to run for Furillo. Dodger manager Burt Shotton then unexplicably ordered Gionfriddo to steal second base. This maneuver could have easily ended the game, but catcher Yogi Berra's throw was high, and Gionfriddo slid in safely under the tag.

Yogi's hitting prowess was not to be disputed. He had stroked the first pinch-hit home run in a World Series on the previous afternoon.

However, he had not yet developed the talent that would eventually make him a Hall of Fame catcher.

With Pete Reiser batting for the pitcher, Yankee manager Bucky Harris made his contribution to the unexplainable by ordering his pitcher to intentionally walk Reiser. The free pass made him the tenth Dodger to stroll to first. Walking the potential winning run is a no-no, and in this case, it cost the Yankees the ball game.

Lavagetto stepped up to the plate and proceeded to smack the ball. The drive chased right-fielder Tommy Henrich back to the scoreboard. Henrich could only watch helplessly as the ball caromed off the wall, away from his desperate reach. As he finally retrieved the pellet, the two speedy runners had crossed the plate.

Later when Bevens fielded post-game questions from the press about his reaction to the disappointing and shocking climax, he stated that he was not even aware he was pitching a no-hitter. Because of his wildness, Bevens observed so many runners on base, he only hoped to win the game. Lavagetto ruined his hopes for the victory and the no-hitter with one swing of his bat.

DODGERS-YANKEES RECAP

	R	H	E
Brooklyn	3	1	3
New York A	2	8	1

Winning pitcher- Casey
Losing pitcher- Bevens
Home runs- none

HERO * Lavagetto
GOAT < Berra

1948

MAJOR HEADLINES

The Soviet Union institutes a land blockade of all Allied sectors of the divided city of Berlin. The United States and Great Britain counter with the Berlin Blockade by dropping packages of food, clothing, medical supplies, and other valuables into the city from the air.

Former State Department official Alger Hiss is indicted for perjury after he denies having passed secret documents to the Russians.

Harry Truman upsets heavily favored Thomas E. Dewey to win re-election to another term as president.

SPORTS

Baseball- Cleveland Indians defeat Boston Braves in six games in the World Series.

Pro Football- Philadelphia Eagles win NFL title by defeating the Chicago Cardinals.

College Football- Michigan is voted the National Champion.

Pro Basketball- Baltimore Bullets over the Philadelphia Warriors in the NBA finals.

College Basketball- Kentucky defeats Baylor in the NCAA finals.

Hockey- Toronto defeats Detroit to win the Stanley Cup.

U.S. Open Tennis-
    Men's finals: Pancho Gonzales defeats Eric Sturgess
    Women's finals: Margaret Osborne duPont defeats Louise Brough

MOVIES- ACADEMY AWARDS

Best Actor: Laurence Olivier, *Hamlet*
Best Actress: Jane Wyman, *Johnny Belinda*
Best Director: John Huston, *Treasure of the Sierra Madre*
Best Picture: *Hamlet*

CHAPTER III
A MOST UNHAPPY FELLER

Wednesday, October 6, 1948- Braves Field, Boston, MA
World Series Game One, Boston Braves 1, Cleveland Indians 0

When the National League Boston Braves won the pennant, and the American League Red Sox tied the Cleveland Indians for first, New England fans were anxiously hoping that the 1948 World Series would be an all-Boston affair. The Indians, however, foiled their hopes by trouncing the Red Sox in a one-game playoff at Boston's Fenway Park.

In the opening game of the Series at the other Boston playing site, Braves Field, an extremely questionable umpiring call enabled the Braves to edge Cleveland 1 to 0. Boston scored the only run of the game in the eighth inning, as future Hall-of-Famer Bob Feller suffered a heartbreaking defeat.

The game was a mound duel between Feller and another outstanding right-hander, Johnny Sain. Neither side came close to scoring for the first seven innings. In the home eighth, a base on balls, only the second walk Feller issued all day, was the premonition of doom for the Indians.

A sacrifice and an intentional walk left runners on first and second with two out, when one of the most controversial plays in World Series history would decide the outcome.

The Cleveland shortstop and player-manager, Lou Boudreau, slowly snuck behind the runner at second, Phil Masi. Masi had boldly been taking a lead off the base, but as Boudreau reached second, Feller whirled and quickly threw toward the bag. The play appeared to work perfectly, as Boudreau snared the ball and slapped the tag on Masi as he dove head-first back to the base. The classic pick-off attempt had worked successfully many times during the season, and once again it appeared that the Indians would escape undamaged.

When umpire Bill Stewart flashed the "safe" sign, the entire Cleveland team stared in shock and incredulous disbelief. Without the Instant Replays that now exist, no one could verify Stewart's costly blunder.

Instead of the inning concluding, the Indians were forced to secure a fourth out. The next batter, Tommie Holmes, then lined a single to left to drive in Masi with the winning run.

Although both hurlers produced outstanding efforts, Feller lost his only opportunity to ever win a World Series game, which was his lifelong dream. He allowed only two hits, including Holmes' game-winner. Sain was equally brilliant for Boston. He gave up four hits but didn't walk a batter.

After reviewing the play on film for more than five decades, no one can justify the umpire's blown call. It still seems impossible that Masi eluded Boudreau's tag and safely touched second base. The Tribe was fortunate that the umpiring decision only cost them one game. They took the '48 Series in six games and have yet to win another championship since that time.

BRAVES-INDIANS RECAP

	R	H	E
Boston N	1	2	2
Cleveland	0	4	0

Winning pitcher- Sain
Losing pitcher- Feller
Home runs- none

HEROES ** Sain, Holmes
GOAT < Bill Stewart (umpire)

<u>1949</u>

MAJOR HEADLINES

The North Atlantic Treaty Organization (NATO) is established. The United States, Canada, and ten Western European countries join forces to agree to protect any participating nation against armed attack.

The infamous Japanese wartime broadcaster, Tokyo Rose, is given a ten-year prison sentence for treason.

Eleven U.S. Communist party leaders are convicted of advocating the violent overthrow of the government.

SPORTS

Baseball- Yankees defeat Dodgers in five-game World Series.

Pro Football: Philadelphia wins second straight NFL title from the Los Angeles Rams.

College Football- Notre Dame is voted the National Champion.

Pro Basketball: Minneapolis Lakers defeat the Washington Capitols in the NBA finals.

College Basketball: Kentucky beats Oklahoma State in the NCAA championship.

Hockey: Toronto defeats Detroit in the Stanley Cup finals.

U.S. Open Tennis-
    Mean's Finals: Pancho Gonzales defeats F. R. Schroeder Jr.
    Women's Finals: Margaret Osborne duPont defeats Doris Hart.

MOVIES- ACADEMY AWARDS

Best Actor: Broderick Crawford, *All the King's Men*
Best Actress: Olivia de Haviland, *The Heiress*
Best Director: Joseph Mankiewicz, *Letter to Three Wives*
Best Picture: *All the King's Men*

CHAPTER IV
RED SOX FAIL TO TURN THE PAGE

October 1, 1949- Yankee Stadium, Bronx, NY
Final Saturday of the season- New York Yankees 5, Boston Red Sox 4

After failing to win the American League pennant for the past two years, the powerful Boston Red Sox were anxious to gain admission to the World Series. On the final weekend of the 1949 season, the Bosox were poised to enter the Fall Classic. They had chased the Yankees all summer and finally caught them, assuming the lead during the final week of the campaign.

The cities of New York and Boston have developed one of the best rivalries in sports. The Knicks and Celtics in basketball, and the Yankees and Red Sox in baseball have entertained sports fans for ages. But the riveting competition of 1949 was as good as it ever gets.

As for the two ballparks, the contrast is as different as east-coast and west-coast lifestyles. Yankee Stadium, with its triple-decked tiers, its outfield monuments as a testament to the greatness of its past heroes, and its spacious, green field, stands as a majestic cathedral of American sports culture. The Stadium is truly the "Field of Dreams" and a major tourist attraction for out-of-town visitors to the Big Apple.

Boston's Fenway Park is just as historic, but half the size of its New York rival. Built in the early part of the twentieth century, the park has an imposing, hitter-friendly left-field wall know as the Green Monster. It is one of the oldest ballparks in the country. Although Fenway Park is a charming relic from the past, its fans are rabid and knowledgeable, and come from all over New England to fill the cozy little ball park on a daily basis.

The teams were scheduled to meet head-to-head in the final two games at Yankee Stadium to decide the title. As the adversaries squared off on this pleasant Saturday afternoon, the Sox led the Yanks by a game. Furthermore, the Beantowners had their two aces, twenty-five game winner Mel Parnell and twenty-three game winner Ellis Kinder, well-rested and ready to take on the New Yorkers. They only needed to win one of the pair to take the flag.

The players' wives, who made the short train trip from Boston, were prepared to celebrate with their husbands and enjoy the Manhattan night life after the game. When the Red Sox bolted to a 4 to 0 lead in the third inning, their clubhouse started to prepare the champagne.

The Bosox, however did not anticipate that the Yankees' ace reliever, Fireman Joe Page, would come out of the bullpen for the sixtieth time and hurl six and two-thirds innings of scoreless baseball, or that light-hitting outfielder Johnny Lindell would belt the game-winning homerun.

The New York starter, the usually dependable Allie Reynolds, couldn't locate the plate, and his wildness led to an early trip to the showers. In the first inning, he wild-pitched two base runners into scoring position, and an outfield fly netted Boston's first run.

In the third, Reynolds walked the bases loaded and allowed a bloop hit to hand the Red Sox their second run. The Fireman answered the call to the pen and promptly walked the first two batters he faced to put the Sox up by four.

After that dubious start, the southpaw reliever settled down and put out the fire. Boston would not cross home plate again this afternoon.

Meanwhile the Yankees pecked away in the fourth and fifty stanzas. In the fourth, the Bombers netted a pair of runs on three solid hits and an outfield fly. They tied the score in the fifth on four consecutive hits off Parnell. The fourth safety, struck by Yankee star Joe DiMaggio, tied the game and knocked out the left-hander.

The game continued with the score knotted until the home eighth. After the first two batters went down, Johnny Lindell came to bat. In Manager Casey Stengel's strict platoon system, Lindell, whose average stood at a paltry .229, would normally play only when the opposing pitcher was left-handed. Since a right-hander, Joe Dobson, had replaced Parnell, the normal move would be to pull a good lefty hitter such as Gene Woodling off the bench.

Woodling was the other member of Stengel's left-field platoon. However, Casey was also a man of hunches, and this time he played one of those hunches by allowing Lindell to bat. The left-fielder rewarded his faith by crushing the first pitch into the left-field seats to give the Bombers a lead they wouldn't relinquish.

As the frustrated visitors took their ninth turn at bat, Joe Page still toiled on the mound. Although using a reliever for more than an inning or two is unheard of today, the Fireman was starting his seventh inning of work. The Red Sox went down without a whimper, ending the game and canceling their planned celebration.

The win enabled the Yankees to tie the Red Sox for first going into the final meeting on Sunday, a game they would also win on a pop-fly double with the bases loaded that landed on the foul line and cleared the bases.

The Boston Red Sox were becoming extremely proficient at finding ways to lose. Once again they had managed to turn certain victory into agonizing defeat.

YANKEES-RED SOX RECAP

	R	H	E
Yankees	5	12	0
Red Sox	4	4	0

Winning pitcher- Page
Losing pitcher- Dobson
Home run- Lindell

HEROES ** Page, Lindell
GOAT < Dobson

1950

MAJOR HEADLINES

President Truman authorizes the United States to produce the first Hydrogen Bomb.

A Brinks express office in Boston is robbed of $2.8 Million.

President Truman orders American forces to Korea after North Korean troops cross the South Korean border and invade that democratic nation.

The Army seizes control of all railroads on orders from the president in order to avoid a nationwide strike.

SPORTS

Baseball- Yankees sweep the Philadelphia Phillies in the World Series.

Pro Football- Cleveland Browns win their first NFL title by beating Los Angeles.

College Football- Oklahoma is voted the National Champion.

Pro Basketball- Minneapolis defeats Syracuse to repeat as NBA champs.

College Basketball- City College of New York (CCNY) becomes the only team to ever win both the NCAA and NIT championships.

Hockey- Detroit Red Wings defeat the New York Rangers in the Stanley Cup finals.

U.S. Open Tennis-
    Men's finals: Arthur Larsen defeats Herbert Flam.
    Women's finals: Margaret Osborne duPont defeats Doris Hart.

MOVIES- ACADEMY AWARDS

Best Actor: Jose Ferrer, *Cyrano de Bergerac*
Best Actress: Judy Holliday, *Born Yesterday*
Best Director: Joseph Mankiewicz, *All About Eve*
Best Picture: *All About Eve*

CHAPTER V
ASHBURN SAVES THE DAY

Sunday, October 1, 1950- Ebbets Field, Brooklyn, NY
Final day of the season- Philadelphia Phillies 4, Brooklyn Dodgers 1,
(10 innings)

In a thrilling conclusion to the 1950 season, the Philadelphia Phillies won their second National League pennant, and first in thirty-five years, by outlasting the challenge of the Brooklyn Dodgers 4 to 1 in ten innings at Ebbets Field in Brooklyn. The Phillies won the game they had to win with their right-handed ace, Robin Roberts, hurling ten gallant innings for his twentieth victory.

With ten days remaining in the season, the Philllies were cruising towards the title. They lead second-place Boston by six games, and the favored Dodgers trailed by a distant nine markers in third place.

As the campaign entered the homestretch, the Phils' worst slump of the season coincided with the surge of the Dodgers. The Brooks moved to within two games of Philadelphia as the clubs prepared to square off in the final two games at the old neighborhood ballpark in Flatbush..

When Brooklyn won the Saturday contest, the season came down to one game If the Dodgers could defeat the team from the City of Brotherly Love again, the teams would tie for first, thus forcing a three-game playoff beginning the next day in Brooklyn. With the Dodgers having the momentum, the Flatbush club would be heavy favorites to capture the playoff and cop the flag.

The Sunday game offered a mound duel between Roberts and the ace righty of the Dodgers, Don Newcombe. Since parking was limited at Ebbets Field, most of the sellout throng flocked to the game by bus, trolley, or even on foot.

The teams matched zeros for five innings, but in the sixth, Philadelphia managed to bunch three of its eleven hits to draw first blood. Brooklyn rebounded for a run in its turn to knot the count, as Peewee Reese smacked a homer over the right field scoreboard.

The tension continued to mount as the game entered the home ninth. Ballgame sponsors on radio and TV were almost entirely beer and tobacco products, which the patrons could purchase at the park.

Thus many of the 35,000 fanatics were sitting on the edge of their seats drinking their Schaefers and puffing their Old Golds.

The first two Dodgers reached base, and the fans prepared to celebrate. Duke Snider was the next batter, and he lined the first pitch into center field for a base hit. The runner on second base, a hometown boy named Cal Abrams, received the green light at third base and raced toward home plate carrying the winning run.

Center-fielder Richie Ashburn, a future Hall of Famer, who would not reach Cooperstown because of his throwing arm, got to the ball quickly and rifled a perfect strike to the plate. His throw to catcher Stan Lopata nailed Abrams by ten feet. The runner didn't help the situation by taking an unusually wide turn around third base.

With the dangerous Jackie Robinson due up and first base open, the Phils logically put Robby on to load the bases, but neither Carl Furillo nor Gil Hodges could drive in the runner from third. Roberts had dodged the bullet, and the nail-biter went into extra innings.

In the visitors' tenth, Roberts helped his own cause by leading off with a single. With two out, another safety put runners at first and second. The batter was Dick Sisler, the son of the legendary baseball immortal, George Sisler. He lofted a home run into the left field seats to silence the crowd and punctuate the season. The homer, Sisler's fourth hit of the day, was the most notable of his career. As the Dodgers went down meekly in the final round, the Phils jubilantly savored a most remarkable victory.

The Phillies were extremely proud of their accomplishments in 1950. Despite slumping in the final month of the season, they pulled themselves together, and with courage and determination refused to allow themselves to lose the most important game in their history.

PHILLIES-DODGERS RECAP

	R	H	E
Philadelphia	4	11	0
Brooklyn	1	5	0

Winning pitcher- Roberts
Losing pitcher- Newcombe
Home runs- Reese, Sisler

HEROES *** Ashburn, Roberts, Sisler
GOAT < Abrams

1951

MAJOR HEADLINES

Senator Estes Kefauver leads a Senate investigation into Organized Crime.

President Truman relieves General Douglas Mac Arthur from his command in Korea for defying orders.

Coast-to-coast live television transmission is inaugurated.

SPORTS

Baseball- Yankees defeat Giants in six games in all-New York World Series.

Pro Football- LA Rams win NFL title from the Cleveland Browns.

College Football- National Champion is Tennessee.

Pro Basketball- Rochester Royals defeat the NY Knickerbockers for the NBA title.

College Basketball- Kentucky defeats Kansas State in the NCAA finals.

Hockey- Toronto Maple leafs defeat the Montreal Canadiens in an all-Canada Stanley Cup Final.

U.S. Open Tennis-
    Men's Finals: Frank Sedgman defeats E. Victor Seixas Jr.
    Women's Finals: Maureen Connolly defeats Shirley Fry.

MOVIES- ACADEMY AWARDS

Best Actor: Humphrey Bogart, *The African Queen*
Best Actress: Vivian Leigh, *A Streetcar Named Desire*
Best Director: George Stevens, *A Place in the Sun*
Best Picture: *An American in Paris*

CHAPTER VI
A GIANT MIRACLE

Wednesday, October 3, 1951 – Polo Grounds, New York, NY
National League Playoff Game 3- New York Giants 5, Brooklyn Dodgers 4

The New York Giants spent the entire 1951 season chasing the Brooklyn Dodgers and finally caught them during the final week of the season. The National League pennant race ended with both teams in a first-place tie. For the second time in history, a best two-out-of-three playoff would produce the club that advanced to the World Series.

The two squads not only shared a city, they also shared an intense dislike for each other. Their fiery manager, Leo Durocher, constantly baited the Dodger players from the bench and almost drew equally volatile players like Carl Furillo and Don Newcombe into fights several times.

Likewise the fans of both clubs exhibited similar militant behavior towards each other. They would sometimes get into fistfights over issues like arguing who was the better center-fielder, Duke Snider or Willie Mays. As the Civil War was the War Between the States, this tiebreaker series promised to be the War Between the Boroughs.

The Giants won a close first game, but the Dodgers bounced back to decisively win the second encounter. The decision on who would become the National League champion now rested with a third game tiebreaker to be played at the Giants' home field, the horseshoe-shaped Polo Grounds in Harlem.

This misshapen field had short four lines, where a putting iron could drive the ball into the seats. However, it sloped sharply into a deep center field, where the homerun target extended to almost 500 feet. Furthermore, the clubhouse stood at the end of the playing area in center, and both the winning and losing teams had to walk side-by side across the field on their way to their lockers.

Durocher started his righty ace, Sal "The Barber" Maglie. Maglie was so known because of the close shaves he threw at the chins of opposing batters to keep them from crowding the plate.

Dodger skipper Chuck Dressen countered with Don Newcombe. The Brooks drew first blood in the opening frame, as Jackie Robinson singled in a run.

The New Yorkers broke through to tie in the seventh. Third-baseman Bobby Thomson, who was to become one of the legendary sports heroes of all time, drove in the run with a sacrifice fly.

It was, however, in the Brooklyn eighth that it looked like the end of the line for the Polo Grounders. Maglie surrendered four hits and a walk, and the Dodgers forged a three-run lead that they carried into the bottom of the ninth.

The Giant surge, which produced thirty-nine wins in their final forty-seven games, appeared to have ended. But when the first two batters, Alvin Dark and Don Mueller, led off with hits, Giant fans still had hope. After Monte Irvin fouled out, Whitey Lockman's double drove in a run and drove Newcombe out of the game. On the play, Mueller broke his ankle sliding into third and had to be removed from the field on a stretcher.

Thus one of the most dramatic moments in sports history was about to occur. Clint Hartung replaced Mueller as the runner at third base and Lockman held his place at second. Since the term, "Closer," was not part of the baseball vocabulary of the time, Dressen summoned Ralph Branca, the starter and loser of the first playoff game, from the bullpen to put out the fire.

The first hitter Branca had to face was Bobby Thomson. If Thomson could extend the rally, the on-deck batter would be the outstanding but nervous rookie, Willie Mays. But Willie didn't have to worry. Thomson promptly lined a pennant-winning home run into the left field seats. Giants' announcer, Russ Hodges, who was broadcasting in the WMCA radio booth, screamed, "The Giants win the Pennant," five times before losing his voice and finally yielding the microphone. The Giants had indeed won the pennant, taking a 5 to 4 decision on Bobby Thomson's historic wallop.

The Giants won the 1951 flag against the most overwhelming odds. In April they lost eleven in a row to tumble into the cellar. By August 11, they were a seemingly hopeless thirteen and a half games behind the Dodgers.

Their miraculous pace in the final six weeks enabled them to force a tie as the season ended. In the deciding playoff game, they fell behind by three runs as they came up for their last licks. Then Bobby Thomson belted the "Shot Heard Round the World" as the writers named it, and the Giant miracle was complete.

GIANTS-DODGERS RECAP

	R	H	E
Giants	5	8	0
Dodgers	4	8	0

Winning pitcher- Jansen
Losing pitcher- Branca
Home run- Thomson

HERO * Thomson
GOAT < Branca

1952

MAJOR HEADLINES

President Truman orders seizure of all U.S. steel mills in order to avert a nationwide strike.

The United States, Great Britain, France, and West Germany negotiate a peace contract.

The United States detonates the first Hydrogen device in the Pacific.

Dwight D. Eisenhower soundly defeats Adlai E. Stevenson to become the first Republican president in twenty-four years.

SPORTS

Baseball- Yankees defeat the Brooklyn Dodgers in seven games for their fourth straight World Championship.

Pro Football- Detroit Lions defeat the Cleveland Browns for the NFL title.

College Football: Michigan State is voted the National Champion.

Pro Basketball- Minneapolis Lakers over the New York Knicks for the NBA title.

College Basketball- Kansas defeats St. Johns in the NCAA final.

Hockey- Detroit Red Wings defeat Montreal in the Stanley Cup finals.

U.S. Open Tennis-
    Men's finals: Frank Sedgeman defeats Gardnar Malloy
    Women's finals: Maureen Connolly defeats Doris Hart.

MOVIES- ACADEMY AWARDS

Best Actor: Gary Cooper, *High Noon*
Best Actress: Shirley Booth, *Come Back Little Sheba*
Best Director: John Ford, *The Quiet Man*
Best Picture: *The Greatest Show on Earth*

CHAPTER VII
IT'S UP IN THE AIR

Tuesday, October 7, 1952- Ebbets Field, Brooklyn, NY
World Series Game Seven, New York Yankees 4, Brooklyn Dodgers 2

Only one major league team had won four consecutive World Series before 1952. The New York Yankees of 1936 to 1939 accomplished this feat, and now the Yankees of 1952 were attempting to duplicate their predecessors.

After winning the Series in 1949, 1950, and 1951, the Yanks were shooting for a fourth straight World Championship. Their opponents would be the Brooklyn Dodgers, whom they had already beaten in three previous October Classics. In fact the Dodgers were making their sixth trip to the Series without having earned a victory.

The Flatbush club was now in position to bring the first World Series banner to Brooklyn and end the Yankees' October winning streak. After five games, they led three games to two. All they had to do was win one of two possible matches in the intimate surroundings of their home ball park, Ebbets Field.

The Brooklyn fans prepared for one of the biggest celebrations the borough would ever experience. All the Dodgers had to do was win a baseball game. Since many of the fans lived near the park, those that eschewed the trolley ride enjoyed the walk to the game on a pleasant, sunny autumn afternoon. The site of the famous rotunda at the Ebbets Field entrance excited the Flatbush Faithful, who couldn't wait for the contest to begin.

Brooklyn fans often referred to their heroes as "Dem Bums," and these Bums were hard to beat at home. That is why, even though the Yankees edged them in Game Six, they could not conceive of the team losing two in a row to anyone on their home field.

Both teams were loaded with outstanding starting pitching, and before this game concluded, each squad would trot out all of their best pitchers in an effort to prevail. Dodger manager Chuck Dressen would use his aces, Joe Black, Preacher Roe, and Carl Erskine, while Yankee skipper Casey Stengel would employ Eddie Lopat, Vic Raschi, and

Allie Reynolds. Everyone was available, since they had six months to rest before the next game.

The rivals matched scores in the fourth and fifth frames. Johnny Mize drove in a run, but the Brooks squandered a big opportunity in their half. They loaded the bases with nobody out but could only score once on a sacrifice fly by Gil Hodges. The popular first-baseman symbolized the Brooklyn frustration, as he went hitless throughout the Series.

Gene Woodling homered in the Yankee fifth, but the Dodgers immediately retaliated. Bill Cox doubled and Peewee Reese singled to once again square the count.

The New Yorkers then broke the deadlock in the sixth stanza, as Yankee muscle man, Mickey Mantle, clouted a long homer that cleared the right field screen and presented a pedestrian on Bedford Avenue with a valuable souvenir. The Mick, who was having a tremendous World Series, again drove in a run in the seventh with a single.

The home seventh brought the tense struggle to its ultimate climax. The potent-hitting Dodgers once again loaded the bases with only one out. With lethal batters like Duke Snider and Jackie Robinson due up and the Yankees "Big Three" mound stars already having run out of gas, Stengel brought in a seldom-used southpaw named Bob Kuzava to pitch to the lefty-swinging Snider.

Kuzava got the Duke to pop up for the second out, but next up would be Robinson. Jackie lofted another high pop up toward second base. Billy Martin started in for what at first appeared to be a routine chance. The ball, however, became caught in the brisk October winds, which carried it toward home plate. With all three runners racing at full speed and everyone in the ballpark holding his breath, Martin raced past the pitcher's mound, lunged, and caught the ball at his shoe tops to retire the side.

Kuzava worked an easy eighth and ninth to gain the most important save of his career. The New York Yankees were World Champions in each of the first four years of Casey Stengel's managerial reign, something no manager had ever before accomplished.

The Brooklyn Dodgers, who had suffered agonizing losses in the final game of the '50 season and the deciding game of the '51 playoff, now relived the agony of defeat once again in 1952. This time it was not a home run that cost them the title, but a wind-blown pop fly that came within six inches of striking the ground and clearing the bases.

YANKEES-DODGERS RECAP

	R	H	E
NY Yankees	4	10	4
Bkln Dodgers	2	8	1

Winning pitcher- Reynolds
Losing pitcher- Black
Save- Kuzava
Home runs- Woodling, Mantle

HEROES *** Mantle, Kuzava, Martin
GOAT < Hodges

1953

MAJOR HEADLINES

France receives $60 Million from the United States to aid fighting in Indochina.

Julius and Ethel Rosenberg are executed in the Electric Chair for conspiracy to commit Espionage.

An Armistice ends three years of bloody fighting in Korea.

SPORTS

Baseball- Yankees again take the World Series from the Dodgers for a record-setting fifth straight World Series championship.

Pro Football- Detroit repeats as NFL champion by edging Cleveland by one point.

College Football- Maryland is voted the National Champion.

Pro Basketball- The Lakers again defeat the Knicks for the NBA title.

College Basketball- Indiana over Kansas NCAA final.

Hockey- Montreal defeats the Boston Bruins in the Stanley Cup finals.

U.S. Open Tennis-
    Men's Finals: Tony Trabert defeats E. Victor Seixas Jr.
    Women's Finals: Maureen Connely defeats Doris Hart.

MOVIES- ACADEMY AWARDS

Best Actor: William Holden, *Stalag 17*
Best Actress: Audrey Hepburn, *Roman Holiday*
Best Director: Fred Zinneman, *From Here to Eternity*
Best Picture: *From Here to Eternity*

CHAPTER VIII
THE DRIVE FOR FIVE

Monday, October 5, 1953- Yankee Stadium, Bronx, NY
World Series Game Six, New York Yankees 4, Brooklyn Dodgers 3

Second-baseman Billy Martin, whose game-saving catch helped the New York Yankees capture their fourth consecutive World Series Championship in 1952, drove in the game-winning hit enabling the New Yorkers to win an unprecedented fifth straight Series in 1953. Never before and never again has a baseball team won five straight World Titles. The "drive for five" didn't come easily though for the Bombers.

Their opponents were the Brooklyn Dodgers in a rematch of the '52 Series. The Dodgers of 1953 once again featured powerful sluggers Roy Campinella, Gil Hodges, Jackie Robinson and Duke Snider. They easily won the National League pennant and were favored to dethrone the Bronx Bombers. However, the Dodgers trailed the Yankees three games to two, as the intra-city rivals prepared to do battle in Game Six. The scene for this contest and, if necessary the seventh, would be a familiar site, spacious Yankee Stadium.

Injuries to his pitching staff forced Brooklyn manager Chuck Dressen to start his top hurler, Carl Erskine, with only two days rest. Erskine had set a World Series record in his prior start by striking out fourteen batters, but injuries to other starters forced Dressen to send the right-hander to the mound without the proper rest.

The Yankees countered with their premier southpaw, Whitey Ford, whom the Brooks had shelled in his last start. Ford was not comfortable pitching against the predominately right-handed lineup in cozy Ebbets Field but looked to fare better in the big ball orchard in the Bronx.

The New Yorkers gained a quick three-run advantage in the first two innings, but could have put away the contest if not the Whitey Ford's base-running blunder. With the overworked Erskine struggling early in the match, the Bombers lead 3 to 0 and had the bases loaded in the second frame with only one out.

The batter was the ever-dangerous Yogi Berra. Yogi lofted a towering fly deep to center that Snider ably caught up to. It appeared that Whitey could have trotted home, but the surprised Dodgers saw the Duke throw the runner out at the plate. Ford later explained that, on this very overcast afternoon, he couldn't see Snider catch the ball, left third base too soon, and had to go back to tag up. When he arrived at the plate, Campinella waited with the ball in his mitt, which retired the side.

Brooklyn only managed to score once in the sixth. The skillful Jackie Robinson manufactured the run with his hitting and speed. Jackie doubled, stole third, and scored on an infield out. The Dodgers trailed 3 to 1 as their last chance arrived in the climactic ninth inning.

Casey Stengel played one of his unpredictable hunches by bringing in his top quality starter, Allie Reynolds. Reynolds was part Indian by heritage, but on the mound he was all-Yankee. The Chief was the opening-game starter but hurt his back and made only one appearance after that. He retired the Dodgers in the ninth inning to save the fifth game, putting the Yanks on the brink of victory. This time Reynolds could not duplicate his previous efficiency. With one away, Snider singled. Carl Furillo, not one of the main power guys but only the National League batting champion, then sliced a home run into the right field seats to tie the score. Instead of celebrating, the tie forced the disappointed Yankees to bat in the home ninth.

Hank Bauer's walk and Mickey Mantle's hit placed the winning run in scoring position. Bauer and Mantle set the table for Billy Martin to step up to the plate. The feisty second-sacker had done it all in this World Series, a base-clearing triple, two home runs, eleven hits, and flawless defense.

Martin was always one of Stengel's favorite players. Casey admired his aggressive style of play and often referred to him as "Billy the Kid."

Now with a 1-1 count against reliever Clem Labine, The Kid lined the next pitch over second base to almost single-handedly win the game and the World Series. Martin's twelve hits set a record for a six-game Series and tied the all-time World Series hit parade.

The Yankees' World Series victory in 1953 was perhaps their most gratifying. The five consecutive banners have never been equaled. The club always seemed to find a timely hit or strikeout when needed. Casey Stengel managed like a magician. He always seemed to use the right player at the right time in the right position.

The Brooklyn Dodgers failed in their seventh attempt to capture a World Series crown. The Flatbush fans were becoming accustomed to watching a highly talented squad that was the best in its league. But when it attempted to be the best in baseball, the New York Yankees stood in their way, a perennial roadblock. The cry of "wait till next year" continued to echo throughout the borough of Brooklyn, and those anguished cries could be heard all the way to the Bronx.

YANKEES-DODGERS RECAP

	R	H	E
Yankees	4	13	0
Brooklyn	3	8	3

Winning pitcher- Reynolds
Losing pitcher- Labine
Home run- Furillo

HERO * Martin
GOAT < Labine

1954

MAJOR HEADLINES

The first atomic submarine called "Nautilus" is launched in Groton, CT.

Senator Joseph McCarthy conducts televised hearings into alleged Communist infiltration of the Army.

The Supreme Court rules that racial segregation in public schools is illegal.

The Southeast Asia Treaty Organization (SETO) is formed.

SPORTS

Baseball- New York Giants sweep Cleveland Indians in World Series.

Pro Football- Cleveland wallops Detroit to win the NFL championship.

College Football- Ohio State and UCLA share the National Championship.

Pro Basketball- Minneapolis defeats Syracuse in NBA finals.

College Basketball- LaSalle defeats Bradley in the NCAA final.

Hockey- Detroit defeats Montreal to win the Stanley Cup.

U.S. Open Tennis:
    Men's Final: E. Victor Seixas Jr. defeats Rex Hartwig.
    Women's Final: Doris Hart defeats Louise Brough

MOVIES- ACADEMY AWARDS

Best Actor: Marlon Brando, *On the Waterfront*
Best Actress: Grace Kelly, *The Country Girl*
Best Director: Elia Kazan, *On the Waterfront*
Best Picture: *On the Waterfront*

CHAPTER IX
AN A-MAYS-ING CATCH

Wednesday, September 29, 1954- Polo Grounds, New York, NY
World Series Game One, New York Giants 5, Cleveland Indians 2 (10 innings)

It was a game that saw one of the most brilliant catches in World Series history. It was a game that ended with one of the shortest home runs in World Series history. The opening game of the 1954 World Series was one of the strangest games ever played, and the contours of the ball park had almost as much to do with the outcome as the teams that competed.

The New York Yankee string of pennants finally ended after five years. The Cleveland Indians unseated the Yankees to represent the American League, while the other New York entry, the Giants, won their second National League flag since the playoff year of 1951. They easily outdistanced the defending NL champion Dodgers in that race.

The Indians of 1954 won a record-setting 111 games, eclipsing by one the legendary 1927 Yankees of Babe Ruth and Lou Gehrig. The Clevelanders were an awesome club and solid favorites to continue the recent American League domination in the October games.

Poetically enough, the World Series opened on a mild Indian Summer afternoon at the Polo Grounds in Upper Manhattan. Cleveland manager Al Lopez named twenty-three-game winner Bob Lemon as his starter. The New Yorkers countered with an equally tough Sal "The Barber" Maglie.

The Indians sent an early message to Giant fans in the very first inning, as first-baseman Vic Wertz lined a monstrous triple to deep right-center field to drive in a pair of runs. The partisan spectators started to squirm in their seats in the rickety old ball park.

Although The Barber didn't have his normally razor-sharp control, he pitched out of several jams to keep the Giants in the game. In their half of the third, they bunched together three hits and a walk culminating in the tying runs. The Clevelanders also squelched several other New York scoring opportunities.

As the visitors batted in the eighth, they determined to end the suspense and put away the game. When the first two batters reached base, the malevolent image of Vic Wertz appeared at the plate. The Giants hadn't retired Wertz all day, and manager Leo Durocher summoned southpaw Don Liddle to face the menacing hitter.

Wertz waited for Liddle's first offering then smacked it to deep center field with tremendous force. Giant fans held their breaths, as their great center-fielder, Willie Mays, raced toward the distant bleacher wall. Running with his back to the plate, Willie looked like Jerry Rice trying to flag down a long pass from Joe Montana in the end zone.

Willie made an over-the-shoulder grab just as he was about to strike the wall. The amazing catch was one of the most remarkable catches not only in a World Series, but in all of baseball history.

The ball traveled over 450 feet, and ironically, it was the only time Giant pitching could retire Wertz all day. He stroked a double, triple, and two singles in his other plate appearances.

After this game-saving play, the contest went into extra innings. The home tenth Saw Lemon still laboring on the mount for the Tribe, when Mays led off with a walk. The brilliant Giant star then stole second, forcing the Indians to intentionally walk the next batter to attempt a double play.

The scheduled hitter, Monte Irvin, would not bat. Durocher reached into his bench and pulled out his extraordinary pinch hitter, Dusty Rhodes. The Polo Grounders had taken the Dusty Rhodes many times during the season, as the powerful lefty had often bailed out his club with clutch hits or homers.

Now he lifted a fly ball down the right field line. Right-fielder Dave Pope raced back to the wall, leaped, but came down with nothing but splinters. The ball landed in the first row of seats just inside the foul pole for a three-run home run, a drive that traveled about 260 feet.

The Giants, in one of their most gritty performances of the year, had defeated the Indians 5 to 2 in a ten-inning classic. The awkward, horseshoe-shaped field had much to do with the outcome. In other major league parks, Vic Wertz would have had three homeruns. Catcher Jim Hegan walloped a drive to left-center field with the bases loaded in the eighth inning that only went for a long out. Elsewhere it would have been a grand slam homer, but since Hegan didn't pull it sharply enough, the fly out only retired the side.

The defeat appeared to demoralize the Cleveland Indians, who went flat like week-old club soda for the rest of the Series. The Giants won the next three games with little resistance, to pull off an astounding four-game sweep. The Indians became victims of a 460-foot drive that was caught and a 260-foot drive that wasn't.

GIANTS-INDIANS RECAP

	R	H	E
New York N	5	9	2
Cleveland	2	8	0

Winning pitcher- Grissom
Losing pitcher- Lemon
Home run- Rhodes

HEROES- ** Mays, Rhodes
GOAT <- None

1955

MAJOR HEADLINES

The United States agrees to help train the South Vietnamese army.

The merger of America's two largest labor organizations is formed under the name of the "American Federation of Labor and Congress of Industrial Organizations." (AFL-CIO)

SPORTS

Baseball- Brooklyn Dodgers defeat the New York Yankees in seven games to win their first World Series.

Pro Football- Cleveland trounces Los Angeles for the NFL title.

College Football: Oklahoma is the National Champion.

Pro Basketball- Syracuse Nationals defeat the Fort Wayne Pistons for the NBA title.

College Basketball- San Francisco beats LaSalle in the NCAA finals.

Hockey- Detroit over Montreal, Stanley Cup finals.

U.S. Open Tennis-
    Men's Finals: Tony Trabert defeats Ken Rosewall.
    Women's Finals: Doris Hart defeats Patricia Ward.

MOVIES- ACADEMY AWARDS

Best Actor: Ernest Borgnine, *Marty*
Best Actress: Anna Magnani, *The Rose Tattoo*
Best Director: Delbert Mann, *Marty*
Best Picture: *Marty*

CHAPTER X
GLEE SHOWS IN BROOKLYN

Wednesday, October 5, 1955- Yankee Stadium, Bronx, NY
World Series Game Seven, Brooklyn Dodgers 2, New York Yankees 0

Next year finally arrived for the Brooklyn Dodgers in 1955. After seven futile attempts at winning the World Series, the Dodgers finally grabbed the brass ring. Their exciting 2 to 0 victory over their perennial tormentors, the New York Yankees, occurred on a sunny afternoon at the familiar postseason site of Yankee Stadium.

Brooklyn manager Walter Alston gave the ball to Johnny Podres. The young lefty had beaten the Yankees in Game Three in Brooklyn 8 to 3. Now in the seventh and deciding game, he hurled a masterful shutout against the formidable Bronx Bombers.

The New York starter was another southpaw, Tommy Byrne. Byrne was the second most effective Yankee pitcher behind Whitey Ford. He pitched well enough to win most games but couldn't overcome Podres' superlative effort and some poor defensive support.

The Brooks gave their pitcher all the runs he would need with single markers in the fourth and sixth frames. First-sacker Gil Hodges drove in both runs. His fourth-inning hit scored Roy Campinella, who had doubled. Then in the sixth, after Moose Skowron's error at first base had loaded the bases, Gil lofted a sacrifice fly to deep center field to plate the second run.

The Bombers, however refused to go down meekly. In the bottom of the sixth, their first two batters reached base, setting up the turning point of the World Series. With the left-handed pull hitter, Yogi Berra, at bat, the Dodger outfield shifted toward right field. Berra swung at an outside pitch and lifted a fly ball down the left-field line.

Left-fielder Sandy Amoros, who was shaded to left-center, had to race toward the foul line. The drive looked like a game-tying double or triple, to everyone except Amoros, that is. Without breaking stride, the swift outfielder reached out and speared the ball just as he reached the foul line. The runner at first base, Gil McDougald, had almost made it to second, and the throw back to the infield easily caught him off base for a double play.

The Amoros Catch was the last opportunity for the New Yorkers to score. When Elston Howard grounded out to shortstop Peewee Reese with two out in the ninth, the Brooklyn Dodgers had found their impossible dream, becoming the World Champions of baseball for the first time.

Just as the Yankees had received all the breaks in their five previous matches with their cross-town rivals, now everything went the Dodgers' way in 1955. After clinching the National League pennant three weeks before the end of the season, the Dodgers lost the first two Series games, and it looked like the same old story. Brooklyn then became the first team in history to bounce back to win a World Series after dropping the first two games.

In the fateful sixth inning, right-hander bob Grim replaced Byrne on the mound. Manager Alston could then return left-fielder Junior Gilliam to his normal position at second base and insert the lefty-swinging Amoros in left field. As fate would have it, Amoros snared Berra's drive, reaching out with his gloved right hand. Gilliam would have had to make a backhand attempt with his left hand and most likely not have made that catch.

The Yankees lost only their fifth World Series in twenty-one efforts. While the fans treated what would become the Dodgers' first and only World Series triumph in Brooklyn with jubilation and glee, the cry of "wait till next year" shifted across the city to the Bronx.

DODGERS-YANKEES RECAP

	R	H	E
Brooklyn	2	5	0
Yankees	0	8	1

Winning pitcher- Podres
Losing pitcher- Byrne
Home runs- none

HEROES ** Amoros, Podres
GOAT < Skowron

1956

MAJOR HEADLINES

Soviet troops crush a revolt in Hungary.

Many Southern Congressmen call for a massive public resistance to the Supreme Court's desegration policy.

The first transatlantic cable is put into operation.

Dwight Eisenhower easily defeats Adlai Stevenson to be re-elected president.

SPORTS

Baseball- Yankees defeat the Dodgers in seven games in the World Series.

Pro Football- New York Giants wallop the Chicago Bears to win the NFL title.

College Football- Oklahoma repeats as the National Champion.

Pro Basketball- Philadelphia Warriors defeat Fort Wayne in the NBA finals.

College Basketball- San Francisco defeats Iowa to repeat as NCAA champion.

Hockey- Montreal beats Detroit in the Stanley Cup finals.

U.S. Open Tennis-
    Men's finals: Ken Rosewall defeats Lewis Hoad.
    Women's finals: Shirley Fry defeats Althea Gibson.

MOVIES- ACADEMY AWARDS

Best Actor: Yul Brenner, *The King and I*
Best Actress: Ingrid Bergman, *Anastasia*
Best Director: George Stevens, *Giant*
Best Picture: *Around the World in Eighty Days*

CHAPTER XI
A PERFECT EFFORT

Monday, October 8, 1956- Yankee Stadium, Bronx, NY
World Series Game Five, New York Yankees 2, Brooklyn Dodgers 0

In the 1956 World Series, the New York Yankees faced the Brooklyn Dodgers for the sixth time in the past ten years. This time however, the situation was slightly different. This time it was the Dodgers who were defending their World Championship and the Yankees who were challenging to recapture the crown.

As the Series moved into the pivotal fifth game with each team having won a pair, the combatants once again prepared to do battle at the imposing Bronx ball yard, Yankee Stadium. In a close Series such as this one, the fifth game is often the most crucial, since it reduces the margin of error for the team that loses to practically zero.

The more than sixty-five thousand people in attendance at the Stadium and the millions more watching on TV or listening on the radio had no idea that they were about to experience an historic sporting event of epic proportions.

The Dodger starter was Sal Maglie, the former Giant star, who at age thirty-nine had made a major contribution to help the Brooks win their second straight pennant. His thirteen victories during the '56 season included a no-hitter, and The Barber won the Series opener with a complete-game 6 to 3 triumph. Maglie had made a skillful transition from pitching against the hated Dodgers to helping them win.

The Bronx club countered with a tall right-hander, Don Larsen. Larsen had won eleven games during the season, but he didn't survive the second inning of Game Two, which Brooklyn won 13 to 8. Larsen had possibly the best stuff of any pitcher on the staff, but he liked to party as much as he liked to work, and as a result, he hadn't lived up to his potential to this point.

Both hurlers appeared to be sharp right from the start. As the game entered the fourth inning, neither club could place a runner on base.

The game moved swiftly. In the home fourth, after both mound men had retired twenty-three straight batters, the Yanks drew first blood on Mickey Mantle's home run.

Since it was now obvious that runs would be scarce on this day, the New Yorkers managed to build an insurance run in the sixth. Larsen helped his own cause with a well-placed bunt that moved Andy Carey, who had led off with a single, into scoring position. Hank Bauer, the steady, clutch-hitting right-fielder, then drove in the run with another one-base knock.

The game continued to move along at a rapid pace. Although Maglie trailed by two runs, he appeared to get stronger in the late innings. Sal finished off the eighth stanza by striking out the side. Larsen, Bauer, and Joe Collins all went down on strikes to send the contest into the ninth inning.

Larsen, pitching successfully with a no-windup delivery, had retired all twenty-four Dodgers he faced. Don was aware that the Flatbush club as always didn't have a weak spot in their batting order, so retiring batters twenty-five through twenty-seven would be the hardest outs of his life.

Carl Furillo flied to right. Roy Campinella grounded to second. Now only one batter stood between Larsen and pitching immortality.

Manager Walt Alston sent up utility outfielder Dale Mitchell to bat for Maglie. With a count of one ball and two strikes, Larsen threw a fast ball at the knees. Up went the right arm of umpire Babe Pinelli, strike three.

Mitchell started to argue that the pitch was low, but Yogi Berra almost bowled him over as he raced toward the mound to jump into Larsen's huge arms. The catcher applied a bear hug to his battery mate, as the Stadium resounded with a cacophony of noise as if it was New Year's Eve in Times Square.

Don Larsen had hurled not only the first no-hitter in World Series history, but the first perfect game in thirty-four years. Not since Chicago White Sox pitcher Charlie Robertson performed this remarkable feat against the Detroit Tigers in 1922 had fans witnessed a perfect game. Overall, major league pitchers had only tossed seven perfect games in history.

As is usually the case with most no-hitters,, Larsen's perfecto did not come without a few close calls. Three outstanding defensive plays by the Yankees prevented any Dodger from reaching base.

In the second frame, Jackie Robinson smacked a vicious grounder to the right of third base. Carey could not retrieve the ball, but he judiciously deflected it towards McDougald. The shortstop rifled a perfect throw to Collins at first to nip Jackie by an eyelash. In the fifth, Gil Hodges belted a long drive to left-center. Mantle got a good jump on the ball and made a fine backhanded catch. The ball would have been out of any other park except Yellowstone, but in the spacious left-center power alley at Yankee Stadium known as "Death Valley," Mantle was able to haul down the prodigious blast.

In the eighth, it was Hodges again who almost broke up the no-no. This time he buzzed a low liner to the left of Carey. The third-baseman lunged and caught the pellet inches off the ground.

The Yankees recaptured the World Championship by defeating the Dodgers in seven games. No one could argue that Don Larsen's perfect effort was the catalyst that made it possible. For Larsen, he could only realize that this was as good as it gets. He couldn't possibly pitch a better game for the rest of his career.

YANKS-DODGERS RECAP

	R	H	E
Yankees	2	5	0
Brooklyn	0	0	0

Winning pitcher- Larsen
Losing pitcher- Maglie
Home run- Mantle

HEROES *** Carey, Mantle, Larsen
GOATS < None

1957

MAJOR HEADLINES

The Soviet launches Sputnik I, the first earth satellite.

Congress approves the first Civil Rights bill for blacks since the Reconstruction era. The bill guarantees voting rights of minorities.

Arkansas governor Orval Faubus calls out the National Guard to bar nine black students from entering a previously segregated high school in Little Rock.

SPORTS

Baseball- Milwaukee Braves edge NY Yankees in seven games in the World Series.

Pro Football- Detroit thrashes Cleveland in NFL title game.

College Football- Auburn and Ohio State share the National Championship.

Pro Basketball- Boston Celtics take first title defeating the St. Louis Hawks.

College Basketball- North Carolina over Kansas, NCAA final.

Hockey- Montreal repeats as Stanley Cup champion by defeating Boston.

U.S. Open Tennis-
    Men's Finals: Malcolm Anderson defeats Ashley Cooper
    Women's Finals: Althea Gibson defeats Louise Brough

MOVIES- ACADEMY AWARDS

Best Actor: Alec Guiness, *The Bridge on the River Kwai*
Best Actress: Joanne Wodward, *The Three Faces of Eve*
Best Director: David Lean, *The Bridge on the River Kwai*
Best Picture: *The Bridge on the River Kwai*

CHAPTER XII
A POLISHED ACT

Sunday, October 6, 1957- County Stadium, Milwaukee, WI
World Series Game Four, Milwaukee Braves 7, New York Yankees 5
(10 innings)

The Milwaukee Braves were worried. The Braves were making their first postseason appearance since moving from Boston to Milwaukee in 1953 and didn't want to disappoint their rabid fans with a poor showing in the 1957 World Series.

The Milwaukee fans took to the Braves like a duck takes to water. They constantly filled their new ball park, County Stadium, and never stopped yelling and cheering for their adopted team.

Meanwhile the New York Yankees' appearance in the Series was becoming almost automatic. After splitting the first two games in New York, the Bombers walloped the Braves 12 to 3 in the first World Series game ever played in the state of Wisconsin.

Milwaukee didn't want to fall behind any further after that disheartening defeat, so they entrusted their hopes to their left-handed icon, Warren Spahn. Spahnie lost the Series opener when Whitey Ford bested him 3 to 1 at Yankee Stadium. Now he would be starting the most important game of his magnificent career.

After spotting the Yanks a run in the opening frame, the Braves did what the noisy fans hoped they'd do. They used the long ball to gain a lead they hoped would help them tie up the Series. A pair of round-trippers in the fourth, one by their heralded slugger, Hank Aaron, and another by first baseman Frank Torre, gave the Beer Men four big runs. Aaron's blast came with two men on base.

The National League champs handed over their three-run cushion to Spahn, and it appeared that their trust was well-founded. The contest went into the ninth inning with Milwaukee still holding a comfortable 4 to 1 advantage.

When Spahn retired the first two Yankees and got two strikes on Yogi Berra, it looked like a routinely outstanding win for the great southpaw. Berra, however, never took well to losing. He singled to right, and the next batter, Gil McDougald, followed with another safety.

The next hitter was the versatile Elston Howard. Howard came up to the Yankees as their first African-America player, who was an all-star catcher in the minor leagues. With Yogi behind the plate almost every day, he willingly did whatever his boss, Casey Stengel, asked of him, including performing capably in the outfield or at first base. A good right-handed hitter, Howard was devastating against lefties, even the great ones like Spahn.

When Howard then crushed a Spahn fastball into the left field seats, the stunned crowd, many of whom had started for the exits, returned to their seats. As the macabre short story writer, Edgar Allen Poe, once stated, "The silence was deafening."

The game moved into extra innings, and the Braves began to realize that containing the Yankee players from winning was like trying to stop their loquacious manager from talking. Hank Bauer stretched his World Series hitting streak to eleven games by walloping a triple against the center-field fence to drive in the go-ahead run in the tenth. Bauer hadn't suffered a hitless World Series game since Johnny Podres shut him and the rest of his team out in the seventh game of the '55 Series.

Braves fans sat glumly after seeing certain victory quickly snatched from their grasp. Nippy Jones was the pinch hitter for Spahn in the home tenth. Spahn's second straight World Series defeat now seemed imminent despite two strong efforts.

Stengel gave the ball to his speedy but erratic lefthander, Tommie Byrne, to preserve the victory. Byrne uncorked a wild pitch that appeared to strike the dirt around home plate and rolled all the way back to the stands. Umpire Augi Donatelli at first ruled it a wild pitch. In the acrimonious discussion that followed, Jones called for the ball and showed it to Donatelli, clearly pointing out the polish marks on the ball.

Since baseball players have always had their cleats shined before each game, the umpire observed the black marks on the ball and waved Jones to first. The highly partisan crowd now resuscitated their hopes.

After the pinch-runner, Felix Mantilla, advanced to second on a sacrifice, the drama moved into high gear. Shortstop Johnny Logan doubled to left to once again tie the game.

The crew from the land of bratwurst and beer could not have positioned themselves any better. Their slugging third-baseman, Eddie Mathews, was due up and right behind him, Hank Aaron. Mathews drew a full count on Yankee hurler Bob Grim. He then launched a towering home run into the right field bleachers to end this thrilling game and even the World Series at two games apiece.

The frenetic fans roared with glee and refused to leave the stadium. The Braves rescued themselves from an almost hopeless situation of falling behind the Yankees by two games, placing them on the verge of elimination. Even if they then won the fifth game, they would face the Herculean task of winning two more games in front of a hostile Yankee Stadium crowd.

The fourth game of this outstanding World Series would prove to be the turning point from which the baseball-crazed city of Milwaukee would soon experience its first World Championship.

The game had everything a Braves fan could wish for; home runs by their two super stars, Aaron and Mathews, a Warren Spahn victory, and a come-from-behind win over the hated Yankees. The Milwaukee Braves showed their fans and the nation what an outstanding team can do with spirit, determination, and a little polish.

BRAVES-YANKEES RECAP

	R	H	E
Milwaukee	7	7	0
New York A	5	11	0

Winning pitcher- Spahn
Losing pitcher- Grim
Home runs- Aaron, Torre, Howard, Mathews

HEROES *** Spahn, Mathews
GOATS < Grim, Byrne

1958

MAJOR HEADLINES

The first US Satellite to go into orbit, Explorer One, is launched.

United States Marines are dispatched to Lebanon to protect the government from the threat of an overthrow.

The first domestic jet airline service in the nation is started, with a run between New York and Miami.

SPORTS

Baseball- Yankees defeat Milwaukee in seven games in the World Series.

Pro Football- Baltimore Colts edge NY Giants in the first sudden-death game over played.

College Football- LSU is voted the National Champion.

Pro Basketball- St. Louis Hawks defeat the Boston Celtics for the NBA championship.

College Basketball- Kentucky beats Seattle in the NCAA final.

Hockey- Montreal defeats the Boston Bruins in the Stanley Cup finals.

U.S. Open Tennis-
    Men's Finals: Ashley Cooper defeats Malcolm Anderson.
    Women's Finals: Althea Gibson defeats Darlene Hard.

MOVIES- ACADEMY AWARDS

Best Actor: David Niven, *Separate Tables*
Best Actress: Susan Hayward, *I Want to Live*
Best Director: Vincente Minelli, *Gigi*
Best Picture: *Gigi*

CHAPTER XIII
BRAVE HEART, TIRED ARM

Wednesday, October 8, 1958- County Stadium, Milwaukee, WI
World Series Game Six, New York Yankees 4, Milwaukee Braves 3 (10 innings)

The New York Yankees were desperately seeking revenge against the Milwaukee Braves. The two rivals repeated their exciting 1957 World Series with an encore in 1958.

The Braves were the last National League team to meet the Yankees in October, and when Milwaukee defeated the Yanks in the '57 Series, they became the only National League opponent never to have lost a World Series to the mighty Yankees. Besides, the New Yorkers hadn't lost successive World Series since 1921 and 1922, when their cross-town rivals, the Giants, did the trick. For this reason, they didn't want to be embarrassed by now losing two in a row to the same team again.

After four games, the Braves had a commanding three-to-one lead, and the Yankees' chances of adding Milwaukee to their list of NL victims appeared grim. Warren Spahn's two-hit shutout at Yankee Stadium put the Bronx Bombers on the brink of defeat. Even if they survived a fifth game, the Yanks would have to overcome the Braves twice in the Milwaukee park, County Stadium, where they had so far lost four out of five.

Yankee starter Bob Turley tossed a shutout in game five in New York, sending the Series back to Milwaukee. The Braves considered that an interruption. When they returned home, manager Fred Haney selected Spahn, the tireless immortal, to hurl the clincher with only two days rest. Spahnie had gone ten innings in the opener to beat the New Yorkers 4 to 3. He then shut out the perennial American League champs at the Stadium, setting himself up to become a three-game winner.

Yankee manager Casey Stengel countered with southpaw Whitey Ford. Casey, like Haney, gambled on his ace left-hander with only two days of rest. It was no secret how much each man wanted to win.

The Yanks drew first blood in their initial at-bat. Hank Bauer smoked his fourth home run of the Series. With that clout, the implacable right-fielder joined some rather select company. Only Babe

Ruth, Lou Gehrig, and Duke Snider had ever stroked four homers in a World Series before.

The Braves retaliated against Ford with single markers in the first and second innings. They raked the Yankee star for five hits in an inning and a third. When Spahn, a good-hitting pitcher, singled in the second run, Stengel realized that his Ford was running out of gas. He gave Whitey the early hook before the team suffered any more damage.

Only a dreadful coaching error spared the Yankees from being the victims of a big inning, and no doubt prevented the Brew Crew from ending the Series. With the bases loaded and only one out, reliever Art Ditmar faced Johnny Logan, The shortstop lifted a fly ball into shallow left field. Third-base coach Billy Herman signaled for the runner at third, Andy Pafko, to tag up. When Elston Howard caught the ball, he could almost touch the infielders, His throw to Berra was true, and it easily doubled up Pafko, aborting the rally. If Pafko had remained at third base, a wild Milwaukee celebration for the second straight year might have been only innings away.

The Braves didn't help themselves with some erratic fielding. They committed four errors in this game. Bill Bruton's outfield miscue in the sixth set up the tying run, which scored on Berra's sac fly.

After Ford's shaky start, the Yankees received impeccable work from Ditmar and Ryne Duren out of the bullpen. Neither club could dent home plate through the regulation nine, thus the contest went into extra innings.

The Bombers always managed to find someone to come up with a big hit, so it was in the tenth stanza. This time it was their multi-talented infielder, Gil McDougald, who smashed a lead-off homer off Spahn. When Howard and Berra both smacked two-out singles, Haney sadly relieved his pitching star of duty. Spahn received a thunderous standing ovation as he left the field.

The next batter, Moose Skowron, greeted reliever Don McMahon with the fourth hit of the inning, thus cushioning the New York advantage to 4 to 2.

The feisty Braves, who had overcome a tenth-inning Yankee lead in the '57 Series, now hoped for history to repeat itself. Hank Aaron singled in a run with two out. When first-baseman Joe Adcock rifled another hard smash to center, the Braves had the potential tying run at third, and Adcock was Match Point at first.

Undaunted as ever, Professor Stengel brought in his fire-balling right-hander, Bob Turley. Turley was the Yanks' best pitcher in 1958, an eventual Cy Young winner. Bullet Bob had just hurled a shutout, and now Stengel was asking him to retire one more batter. Yankee fans who remembered the exploits of Harry Brecheen in the 1946 World Series now prayed for the same results.

That batter would be the dangerous pinch-hitter, Frank Torre, who, since he hit from the left side of the plate, was not in the starting lineup against Ford. The partisan crowd pleaded with Torre to either extend the contest or end it with a long hit.

When Torre blooped one into short right field, McDougald raced back on the grass, leaped, and speared the ball just as it was about to drop safely to earth. All this gifted Yankee could do was effectively play every infield position, belt the game-winning home run and as the second-baseman on this day, make the game-saving catch.

The fact that the Bronx Bombers would also capture the deciding seventh game to overcome the seemingly insurmountable three-to-one deficit was in no way the fault of Warren Spahn. All this thirty-seven year old marvel could accomplish in this World Series was to pitch twenty-eight and two-thirds innings in three games. He won two, including a shutout, and pitched into the tenth inning of his losing start. He was remarkable in victory and valiant in defeat.

Spahn did just about everything for the Milwaukee Braves except sell hot dogs. The heart was brave, but the arm nearly fell off.

YANKEES-BRAVES RECAP

	R	H	E
Yankees	4	10	1
Milwaukee	3	10	4

Winning pitcher- Duren
Losing pitcher- Spahn
Home runs- Bauer, McDougald

HEROES *** Duren, Turley, McDougald
GOATS < Bruton, Pafko

<u>1959</u>

MAJOR HEADLINES

Alaska and Hawaii are admitted to the Union as the forty-ninth and fiftieth states.

Soviet Premier Nikita Krushchev visits and tours the United States for the first time.

Fidel Castro leads a rebel band of guerilla fighters in taking over Cuba. The reigning dictator, Fulgencio Batista, is forced to flee the country.

SPORTS

Baseball- Los Angeles Dodgers defeat the Chicago White Sox in a six-game World Series.

Pro Football- Baltimore again defeats the NY Giants in the NFL title game.

College Football- Syracuse is the National Champion.

Pro Basketball- Boston Celtics defeat the Minneapolis Lakers for the NBA title.

College Basketball- California beats West Virginia in the NCAA final.

Hockey- Montreal defeats Toronto to win the Stanley Cup championship.

U.S. Open Tennis-
    Men's Finals: Neale Fraser defeats Alejandro Olmedo.
    Women's Finals: Maria Bueno defeats Christine Truman

MOVIES- ACADEMY AWARDS

Best Actor: Charlton Heston, *Ben Hur*
Best Actress: Simone Signoret, *Room at the Top*
Best Director: William Wyler, *Ben-Hur*
Best Picture: *Ben-Hur*

CHAPTER XIV
A TASTE OF SHERRY

Monday, October 5, 1959- Los Angeles Coliseum, Los Angeles, CA
World Series Game Four, Los Angeles Dodgers 5, Chicago White Sox 4

The World Series of 1959 had a strange cast of unfamiliar faces and a brand new setting. The Yankees had one of their rare off-years and were limited to watching the Series on TV.

The Chicago White Sox, using speed, defense, and solid pitching, won their first American League pennant in forty years. They were as unaccustomed as the Yankees were accustomed to participating in the Fall Classic.

The National League champions were the Dodgers, but not the Brooklyn Dodgers. Team owner Walter O'Malley, whose voracious appetite for cigars, rich food, and an equally rich bank account, had forsaken his Brooklyn roots and led the club to the sunny shores of Southern California. With the Dodgers entrenched in Los Angeles and the Giants relocating to San Francisco, major league baseball had finally become a truly national game.

By winning a pennant in only their second year in LA, the Dodgers brought the World Series to the West Coast for the first time in history. As they prepared for the vital fourth game, the erstwhile Brooks led their Windy City opponents two games to one.

Since they had to find a temporary playing site until their splendid new facility in Chavez Ravine could be completed, O'Malley eschewed the small minor league field in Los Angeles and instead chose the mammoth football stadium, the Los Angeles Memorial Coliseum. The oval field wasn't really suited for baseball, but by redesigning the field with short foul lines and a deep center field similar to the Polo Grounds, the team could squeeze over 90,000 paying customers into O'Malley's Chinese Theatre.

A record crowd of 92,550 jammed into the Coliseum for this all-important fourth game. This represented the largest crowd ever to watch a baseball game anywhere.

The White Sox were struggling to stay alive, while the Dodgers were anxious to end the Series without having to return to Chicago.

Chisox manager Al Lopez entrusted the start to his right-handed ace, Early Wynn. The future Hall-of-Famer had shut out the Angelinos in the opener.

Dodger manager Walter Alston gave the ball to his reliable right-hander, Roger Craig. Craig lost the Series opener, but he was one of the club's most dependable hurlers in clutch situations all season.

When LA broke through for four runs in the home third, it began to look like a long afternoon for the Chicagoans. The White Sox' usually flawless defense deserted them. With two out, the Dodgers struck for five straight hits. Aided by an error by center-fielder Jim Landis and the normally sure-handed shortstop, Luis Aparicio, dropping an outfield relay at second base, the Dodgers found themselves with an early four-run lead. However, with the beckoning left-field screen, no one expected the score to hold. The Coliseum most definitely was a pitcher's nightmare.

Surprisingly the score remained 4 to 0 as the Pale Hose batted in the seventh. Sox bats came to life, and muscular first-baseman Ted Kluszewski drove in their first run with a hard single. With two on and two out, catcher Sherman Lollar came to the plate. Lollar promptly hoisted a fly ball over the short left-field screen attached to the 250-foot foul line. Radio and TV announcers calling games at the Coliseum would often yell, "Screeno!" at this type of home run.

Although disappointed, manager Alston had another ace up his shirt sleeve. He summoned his home-town hero, Larry Sherry, from the bullpen. The righty had saved both Dodger wins and now was appearing in his third consecutive game.

In the home eighth, the popular and long-time Dodger favorite, Gil Hodges, rocketed his fifth World Series homer deep into the left field seats, an authentic home run anywhere. Sherry would not have an opportunity to earn a third save, but by hurling two perfect innings, he became the winning pitcher. The Hollywood Hotshots were a step away from bringing the first World Championship to California.

Hodges had rebounded from the nightmarish World Series in 1952, in which he went hitless. His game-winning four-bagger in this game was one of the most gratifying experiences of his illustrious career.

As for Larry Sherry, the twenty-four-year old Los Angeles native was fast becoming the hero of the Series. What could be more thrilling than winning a championship for your home-town team? The White

Sox had sampled a taste of Sherry that certainly didn't agree with their palates.

DODGERS-WHITE SOX RECAP

	R	H	E
Dodgers	5	9	0
White Sox	4	10	3

Winning pitcher- Sherry
Losing pitcher- Staley
Home runs- Lollar, Hodges

HEROES ** Sherry, Hodges
GOATS < Aparicio, Staley

1960

MAJOR HEADLINES

Nazi war criminal Adolf Eichmann is captured and transported to Israel to stand trial. He is later convicted and executed.

The Russians shoot down a U.S. reconnaissance plane over the Soviet Union and take pilot Gary Powers prisoner.

Vice President Richard Nixon and Senator John Kennedy face each other in the first televised debates of presidential candidates.

Kennedy defeats Nixon by 100,000 popular votes to become the first Roman Catholic to be elected to the presidency

SPORTS

Baseball- Pittsburgh Pirates edge the Yankees in thrilling seven-game World Series.

Pro Football- Philadelphia Eagles edge the Green Bay Packers in the NFL championship.

College Football- Minnesota is voted the National Champion.

Pro Basketball- Boston Celtics defeat the St. Louis Hawks in the NBA finals.

College Basketball- Ohio State defeats California in the NCAA championship game.

Hockey- Montreal defeats Toronto in the Stanley Cup finals.

U.S. Open Tennis-
    Men's Finals: Neale Frasier defeats Rod Laver.
    Women's Finals: Darlene Hard defeats Maria Bueno.

MOVIES- ACADEMY AWARDS

Best Actor: Burt Lancaster, *Elmer Gantry*
Best Actress: Elizabeth Taylor, *Butterfield 8*
Best Director: Billy Wilder, *The Apartment*
Best Picture: *The Apartment*

CHAPTER XV
MAZ, TERRY, AND THE PIRATES

Thursday, October 13, 1960- Forbes Field, Pittsburgh, PA
World Series Game Seven, Pittsburgh Pirates 10, New York Yankees 9

The most surprising thing about the seventh game of the 1960 World Series was that there was a seventh game. The New York Yankees had walloped their National League opponents, the Pittsburgh Pirates, by a combined total of thirty-five runs in their three victories. The Pirates, however, managed to win the other three hard-fought battles by a cumulative six runs.

After taking off the previous Fall, the Yankees had returned to their customary post as American League champions. With sluggers Mickey Mantle and Roger Maris, and the pitching of Whitey Ford and Ralph Terry, the formidable Bronx Bombers were heavy favorites to defeat the Pittsburgh club that won its first pennant since 1927. After thirty-three years of frustration, the city of Pittsburgh embraced its beloved Bucs like never before.

The setting for Game Seven was the old ballpark adjacent to the University of Pittsburgh, Forbes Field. When the game got under way, it looked like the Bucs were serious about pulling off an upset. On a mild Autumn afternoon, the Pirates raked Yankee starter Bob Turley for four runs in the first two innings. First-baseman Rocky Nelson's two-run homer was the big blow that led to Pittsburgh's 4-0 advantage.

Although facing Pirate ace Vernon Law, who had already beaten them twice, they fought back for five runs, four of which came on the strength of circuit clouts by Moose Skowron and Yogi Berra. Yogi's home run, his eleventh in World Series competition, came with two runners on base. His eleven round-trippers tied the brilliant Yankee catcher for third place on the all-time list of career World Series homeruns. Only Babe Ruth and Mickey Mantle had more Series homers.

When New York pushed across another pair of runs in the eighth inning giving them a 7 to 4 lead, it appeared that the Bombers were on their way to their fourteenth World Championship. It was at this point that the ball started to bounce in crazy ways. The next inning and a half defied logic, and not even the most talented Hollywood writer could fashion such a script.

After pinch-hitter Gino Cimoli led off the Pirate eighth with a single, the crucial play of the game and the Series occurred. Centerfielder Bill Virdon hit an apparently routine double-play ball to short. As Tony Kubek readied himself to make the play, the ball, for some unknown reason, bounced up and struck Kubek in the throat. The ball may have struck a pebble in the rock-hard infield, but for whatever reason, Pittsburgh had two on with no one out instead of two out with nobody on. Kubek wound up in the hospital so that doctors could examine his damaged larynx.

After another hit and a sacrifice, the Pirates had drawn a run closer. The dangerous super star, Roberto Clemente, was at bat with runners on second and third. He dribbled a soft grounder between the mound and first. Skowron fielded the ball but was helpless to make a play, since the pitcher, an inattentive Jim Coates, failed to cover the bag. The Pirate eighth was becoming a journey to the Twilight Zone for the Yanks. Instead of being out of the inning with their three-run lead in tact, it was down to a run with two on and only one out. The Yankees were about to pay for their indolence big-time. Catcher Hal Smith, a one-time Yankee farm hand, walloped a three-run home run over the left field wall to give the Bucs a 9 to 7 lead going into the fateful ninth inning.

Although the New York club was shocked by the sudden turnover, it was not yet time to stick a fork into the Yanks. They rallied for three singles to make it a 9 to 8 game. Mickey Mantle drove in the run and sent the potential equalizer to third with only one out.

Another in a series of strange plays in this strange game forced the game to be deadlocked. Mantle showed astute base running alertness, and his quick reaction prevented the contest from ending right there.

Berra hit a sharp ground ball down the first-base line. Nelson grabbed the ball and stepped on the base for the putout. Mantle looked toward second and saw he had no chance to reach the base. Realizing that the force was off since Nelson had already touched first, he smartly darted back to first. As he dove back to the bag, he briskly eluded Nelson's outstretched tag and touched the base. On the play, the tying run scored, and the World Series would become a sudden-death affair.

The lead-off batter in the home half of the ninth would be the Pirates' slick-fielding second-baseman, Bill Mazeroski. No-second-baseman ever turned a double play better than Mazeroski, but now his job was to get on base.

The New Yorkers summoned Ralph Terry from the bullpen as the fifth hurler of the afternoon. Terry was normally the number two starter behind Ford, but in the seventh game of a World Series, all the troops are alerted for duty, since they have all winter to rest.

Terry had good control and threw strikes, one of the reasons Stengel chose him at this vital point. Terry's major fault, however, was his propensity to give up the long ball with some of those strikes. Since Mazeroski was the eighth-place hitter, and with the pitcher's spot up next, and manager Danny Murtaugh running out of players on his bench, Terry seemed like a good bet to carry the Yankees through at least the next two or three innings if necessary.

The first pitch was a ball. On Terry's next delivery, Maz belted a long fly ball that appeared headed toward the left-center field wall. Berra stubbornly ran back toward the barrier but ran out of real estate, as the ball sailed over the wall and into history. For the first time ever, a World Series had ended with a homerun.

The scene reminded knowledgeable observers of Bobby Thomson's clout in the 1951 National League playoff. The delirious Pirate supporters stormed the field. The Pittsburgh Pirates were champions of baseball for first time since 1925. The stunned Yankees slowly walked off the field into their dugout, more shocked than saddened. They couldn't believe they had lost.

Casey Stengel would not return as the manager, but his record, ten pennants and seven World Championships in twelve years, would become a yardstick by which future managers would always be measured.

The final statistics of the '60 Series veiled the outcome. The Yankee batting average of .338 was almost a hundred points better than their opponents. They outscored the Bucs fifty-five to twenty-seven, a two-to-one margin. Their second-baseman, Bobby Richardson, set a World Series record with twelve runs batted in on eleven hits. Richardson's heroics earned him the only World Series Most Valuable Player award for a player from a losing team.

For all the Bombers' statistical dominance, their seventh-game duel with Pittsburgh turned out to be one of the greatest baseball games ever played. When reporters once asked former president Jimmy Carter why he lost his re-election bid to Ronald Reagan in 1980, he succinctly replied that he didn't get enough votes. By this same token, the New York Yankees lost the 1960 World Series because they didn't win enough games.

PIRATES-YANKEES RECAP

	R	H	E
Pittsburgh	10	11	0
New York	9	13	0

Winning pitcher- Haddix
Losing pitcher- Terry
Home runs- Nelson, Skowron, Berra, Smith, Mazeroski

HERO * Mazeroski
GOAT < Terry

1961

MAJOR HEADLINES

The U.S. breaks off diplomatic relations with Cuba.

Cuban exiles' invasion of the "Bay of Pigs" in an attempt to overthrow Fidel Castro is a failure.

Alan B. Shepard Jr. makes the first sub-orbital space flight from Cape Canaveral, FL in a Mercury space capsule.

SPORTS

Baseball- Yankees crush Cincinnati Reds in five games in the World Series.

Pro Football- Green Bay takes the NFL title from the NY Giants.

College Football- Alabama is voted the National Champion.

Pro Basketball- Celtics beat Hawks again in the NBA championship.

College Basketball- Cincinnati wins an all-Ohio NCAA championship from Ohio State.

Hockey- Chicago Black Hawks win the Stanley Cup from the Detroit Red Wings.

U.S. Open Tennis-
    Men's Finals: Roy Emerson defeats Rod Laver.
    Women's Finals: Darlene Hard defeats Ann Haydon.

MOVIES- ACADEMY AWARDS

Best Actor: Maximillian Schell, *Judgment at Nuremberg*
Best Actress: Sophia Loren, *Two Women*
Best Director: Jerome Robins and Robert Wise, *West Side Story*
Best Picture: *West Side Story*

CHAPTER XVI
THE RAJ AND THE BABE

Sunday, October 1, 1961- Yankee Stadium, Bronx, NY
Final Game of the Season, NY Yankees 1, Boston Red Sox 0

A popular philosophy states that, "The more things change, the more they remain the same." So it was with the perennial American League champion New York Yankees.

In 1927 the outstanding Yankee right-fielder was attempting to break Babe Ruth's one-season homerun record on the final day of the season. In 1961 the outstanding Yankee right-fielder was again trying to shatter the Babe's one-season mark on the final game of the season. Each player was part of a team that dominated its league with power, pitching and defense, leaving its rivals behind in a trail of dust.

In 1927 of course, the right-fielder was Babe Ruth himself. The Babe had amassed fifty-nine round-trippers in 1921. On the last game of the '27 season, he had fifty nine, and naturally, he belted his sixtieth in that finale.

In 1961 Yankee right-fielder Roger Maris chased this thirty-four-year-old mark all season and had blasted number sixty on the previous Tuesday. The record that most baseball experts believed would never be broken was on hold for the past five games.

On this summery Sunday afternoon, the crowd filed into Yankee Stadium for this World Series tune-up for the New Yorkers. The right field seats and right-center field bleachers were packed with excited fans hoping to retrieve the historic baseball, should Maris connect.

The Yankee opponents were their traditional rivals, the Boston Red Sox. The Bosox were not a contender in '61, finishing thirty-three games off the pace. But they were participating in an important piece of baseball history. Their starting pitcher, rookie Tracy Stallard, was trying to keep the ball away from Maris' power, much to the dismay of the crowd. He fooled the slugger with an outside pitch on his first at-bat and induced Roger to lift a soft fly ball to left field.

Maris came up for his second plate appearance in the fourth inning. He looked at two pitches that were way off the plate, as the crowd booed lustily.

On Stallard's next delivery, Maris connected and drove the ball on a high, parabolic arc towards right field. The ball landed deep in the seats. Yankee announcer and former great shortstop, Phil Rizzuto, who was broadcasting the game with his usual dramatic flare, shouted "Holy Cow, he did it! Sixty-one home runs for Roger Maris." An ear-splitting roar went up from the stands as Maris circled the bases.

The lucky individual who caught the ball was a nineteen-year-old truck driver named Sal Durante. The youngster was awarded some valuable prizes and another ball that Maris autographed for the youth, all for surrendering the original. Maris tried to tell Durante to keep the ball and get what he could for it, but this was still the Sixties before greed and commercialism became trendy.

His Yankee teammates begged Maris, a normally shy and demure individual, to leave the dugout and acknowledge the request of the fans for a curtain call. Reluctantly he once again appeared on the field, then waved and tipped his cap to the crowd.

The fact that Maris' homerun was the only run of the game meant little to the American League standings. The Yanks won 109 regular-season contests to surpass runner-up Detroit by eight games in Ralph Houk's rookie year as the Yankee manager. Houk was following a tough act in succeeding Casey Stengel at the helm, but his first year was a memorable and highly successful one.

The 1961 Yankees were true Bronx Bombers in every way. They socked 240 home runs, an all-time record at the time. Maris led the club with his sixty-one, followed by Mantle with fifty-four. The Mick was running neck-and-neck with Maris until injuries in the last two weeks of the season forced him out of the lineup. Skowron was third after smashing twenty-eight dingers. Altogether, seven Yankees reached double-figures in homers.

The '61 squad was one of the greatest baseball teams ever assembled. In addition to their raw power, the pitching was superb. Their three top starters, Ford, Terry, and Bill Stafford combined for fifty-five wins.

They had the league's three best catchers, Howard, Berra, (who also saw plenty of outfield duty) and Johnny Blanchard. The trio combined for more than sixty homers and ably handled the pitching staff.

Their wall-to-wall infield of Skowron, Richardson, Kubek, and Clete Boyer was an impenetrable shield, preventing would-be ground balls from going through to the outfield. Mantle and Maris too were among the finest defensive outfielders in the game.

The one bonus for Yankee fans that followed this talented squad all year was the experience of witnessing Roger Maris make history and fulfill his destiny with one swing of his bat.

YANKEES-RED SOX RECAP

	R	H	E
Yankees	1	5	0
Red Sox	0	4	0

Winning pitcher- Stafford
Losing pitcher- Stallard

HERO * Maris
GOAT < Stallard

1962

MAJOR HEADLINES

Lt. Colonel John B. Glenn Jr. circles the earth three times in the Mercury Capsule, Friendship 7, to become the first American to orbit the earth.

James Meredith enters the University of Mississippi as the first black student after Federal troops quell rioting.

President Kennedy orders an air and naval blockade of military weapons shipped to Cuba from the Soviet Union.

SPORTS

Baseball- Yankees defeat San Francisco Giants in a close seven-game World Series.

Pro Football- Green Bay is a repeat winner over the Giants in the NFL championship game.

College Football- Southern California is voted National Champion.

Pro Basketball- Boston defeats the Los Angeles Lakers for the NBA championship.

College Basketball- Cincinnati over Ohio State in NCAA final

Hockey- Toronto defeats Chicago in the Stanley Cup Finals.

U.S. Open Tennis-
    Men's Finals: Rod Laver defeats Roy Emerson
    Women's Finals: Margaret Smith defeats Darlene Hard

MOVIES- ACADEMY AWARDS

Best Actor: Gregory Peck, *To Kill a Mockingbird*
Best Actress: Anne Bancroft, *The Miracle Worker*
Best Director: David Lean, *Lawrence of Arabia*
Best Picture: *Lawrence of Arabia*

CHAPTER XVII
TERRY'S REVENGE

Tuesday, October 16, 1962- Candlestick Park, San Francisco, CA
World Series Game Seven, NY Yankees 1, San Francisco Giants 0

The New York Yankees and San Francisco Giants set a major milestone in 1962, as they participated in the first transcontinental World Series. After relocating from their former New York home in 1958, the Giants managed to capture their first National League pennant since their move to San Francisco. Now the World Series would truly stretch from coast to coast.

The Series was also turning out to be the longest one on record, with four rainouts, one in New York and three in San Francisco. The beautiful city by the bay, which normally experienced its sunniest and warmest month in October, fell victim to a surprising and unseasonable October storm.

This World Series was a hard-fought duel between two squads that alternated wins until a seventh and deciding game at windswept Candlestick Park, the Giants' new home, would decide the championship of baseball. The two starters were right-handed craftsmen, Ralph Terry for the Yanks, and Jack Sanford for the Giants. The two adversaries had opposed each other twice so far, with each winning a game. This match would be the rubber game for the pair, as well as the deciding contest of the Fall Classic.

Both Terry and Sanford appeared to be at their best as the game moved swiftly through four scoreless innings. In the visitors' fifth, the Yankees managed to load the bases with nobody out. Skowron and Boyer both singled, and Sanford committed the cardinal sin of walking the pitcher, as Terry strolled to first base.

Manager Alvin Dark made a decision that, in the long run, would prove costly to the Golden Gaters. He instructed his infielders to play back for a double play and give up a run if necessary. That's exactly what happened, when Tony Kubek grounded into an efficient short-second-first twin-killing. On the play, Skowron scored the go-ahead run.

Again in the eighth, the New Yorkers loaded the bases with no one out. This time reliever Billy O'Dell did an exemplary job of putting out the fire by retiring the Yanks on five pitches without allowing another run to cross the plate.

The ultimate drama would come down to the bottom of the ninth, as the Giants had one last opportunity against Terry. Pinch-hitter Matty Alou led off and surprised everyone with a perfectly-executed drag bunt between the mound and first. Alou remained there as the next two batters struck out.

Terry was still pumped with one out to go. However, his reward for a superlative pitching effort was having to face the two most dreaded hitters in the National League, the two Willies, Mays and McCovey.

Mays lined a hard smash into the right field corner for an obvious double. Then, only the defensive play of the game prevented the tying run from scoring. Showing he was as skilled an outfielder as he was a batter, Roger Maris quickly retrieved the ball in the corner and rifled a bullet back into the infield. Alou wisely held up at third. Had he attempted to score, Roger's throw would have cut him down at the plate to end the Series. Besides, the Giants still had two more menacing bats, McCovey and Orlando Cepeda, ready to drive in the necessary runs.

Terry may have been thinking about his heart-breaking pitch to Bill Mazeroski two years back. He convinced manager Ralph Houk to allow him to pitch to McCovey, confident that he could get him out. The World Series thus became reduced to the most simplistic terms. If McCovey gets a hit, the Giants win. If not, the Yankees win.

On Terry's first delivery, Houk may have regretted his decision. Willie blasted a long drive to right that went foul by about twenty feet. When Terry resumed breathing, he threw another fast ball that McCovey smacked like a bullet over second base. As the ball appeared headed towards right field, Bobby Richardson reached up and speared the streaking pellet. The ball settled in Richardson's glove, and the Giants' last flame of hope had been extinguished. The Yankees had successfully but with extreme difficulty defended their World Championship.

The fact that the only run of the game crossed the plate on a double play indicated the difficulty the Yankees had in finally subduing their stubborn challengers. The San Franciscans were relentless not only in their pursuit of victory in the World Series, but in chasing the Los Angeles Dodgers during the pennant race as well. With one week to go, they trailed the Dodgers by four games, which they made up in the final week of play. They then won the playoff with LA in three games. (memories of 1951)

The win required two fine defensive plays by New York outfielders to cement their victory. In addition to Maris' heroics in the spine-tingling ninth inning, left-fielder Tom Tresh, who would become Rookie of the Year in the American League, made a sparkling grab of a Willie Mays bid for a double in the seventh frame. Tresh raced toward the left-field foul line and back-handed the would-be hit. Since McCovey then stroked a triple into the wind and against the center-field fence, the fine catch by Tresh obviously prevented the tying run from scoring. The catch stranded Willie at third as Cepeda struck out.

As for Ralph Terry, this game vindicated his guilt for throwing the fat gopher against the Pirates in '60. He was the league's best pitcher during the season, winning twenty-three games. His four-hit shutout in the seventh-game thriller gave him two Series victories and earned him the World Series MVP award. The award became a prelude to the Cy Young prize, which the hurler eventually earned as pitcher of the year.

The results of the 1962 World Series show that the New York Yankees won it by a single game. Upon visualizing the ball that smacked into Richardson's glove for the final out, one could better say that the Yankees won the World Series by six inches.

YANKEE-GIANTS RECAP

	R	H	E
Yankees	1	7	0
San Francisco	0	4	1

Winning pitcher- Terry
Losing pitcher- Sanford
Home runs- none

HEROES *** Tresh, Maris, Terry
GOAT < None

1963

MAJOR HEADLINES

President John F. Kennedy is mortally wounded by an assassin's bullet while riding in an open motorcade in Dallas. The accused killer, Lee Harvey Oswald, is later shot and killed in the Dallas County jail by Jack Ruby.

Lyndon B. Johnson is sworn in as president to succeed the slain Kennedy.

The University of Alabama is integrated after Governor George Wallace steps aside.

Civil Rights leader Medgar Evers is assassinated.

A march on Washington is held to support black demands for equal rights.

SPORTS

Baseball- The Los Angeles Dodgers sweep the Yankees in a four-game World Series.

Pro Football- Chicago Bears defeat the Giants for the NFL title.

College Football- Texas is voted the National Champion.

Pro Basketball- Boston is a repeat winner over Los Angeles in the NBA championship.

College Basketball- Loyola of Chicago defeats Cincinnati in the NCAA final.

Hockey- Toronto defeats Detroit in the Stanley Cup finals.

U.S. Open Tennis:
  Men's Finals: Rafael Osuna defeats F.A. Froehling 3rd.
  Women's Finals: Maria Bueno defeats Margaret Smith.

MOVIES- ACADEMY AWARDS

Best Actor: Sidney Poitier, *Lilies of the Field*
Best Actress: Patricia Neal, *Hud*
Best Director: Tony Richardson, *Tom Jones*
Best Picture: *Tom Jones*

CHAPTER XVIII
LOOKING FOR BROOMS IN ALL THE RIGHT PLACES

Sunday, October 6, 1963- Dodger Stadium, Los Angeles, CA
World Series Game Four, Los Angeles Dodgers 2, New York Yankees 1

Beating the New York Yankees in a World Series is difficult enough, but sweeping them in four games—impossible? Not to the Los Angeles Dodgers.

The National League Champs featured some of the most incredible pitching a World Series has ever produced in 1963. The starting trio of Sandy Koufax, Don Drysdale, and Johnny Podres, the hero of the Dodgers' only World Series triumph in Brooklyn back in 1955, had thoroughly shackled the mighty Yankee bats in the first three games, capped by a 1-0 shutout in Game Three by Don Drysdale. The three LA starters limited the Bronx Bombers to three runs and sixteen hits while racing to the 3-0 lead.

Now, on a typically warm, sunny afternoon in Southern California, The Angelinos were ready to bring out the brooms as the fourth and possibly final game was about to start. The capacity crowd at the Dodgers' new pleasure palace, Dodger Stadium, was also hoping that this would be the last baseball game to be played this year.

The new arena had opened the previous year in 1962 and was one of the most picturesque outdoor stadiums in the world. The vista of multi-tiered seats and exotic palm trees standing beyond the outfield bleachers was a photographer's delight. Many a postcard mailed from Los Angeles showed a picture of Dodger Stadium on the front.

The super southpaw, Sandy Koufax was looking to close out the Series. Koufax had set a World Series record in the opener by striking out fifteen Yankees.

Although they had to face the stark realty that no major league team had ever bounced back from a three-zip deficit to take the next four, the New Yorkers were determined to make the Dodgers put away their brooms. They would not concede the war without one last battle.

The Yanks had their own ace ready to challenge the LA club. Whitey Ford was now a crafty veteran of ten previous Octobers. He had become one of baseball's premier pitchers, and after suffering the opening-game defeat, was out for revenge in his return match against Koufax.

Both hurlers appeared to be at their best in the early going. As the mound aces proceeded to mow down batter-after-batter, it appeared that neither would surrender a run.

The outs continued to pile up, and only a pair of long home runs, one from each side, interrupted the reign of batting futility. Outfielder Frank Howard broke the scoreless deadlock with a monstrous home run in the fifth inning. The Dodger behemoth crushed one that soared over the left-field bleachers and half way to San Diego.

In the seventh, Mickey Mantle, whose moon shots were already legend to baseball fans, tried to match Howard's blast. Although the ball didn't travel quite as far as Howard's, it counted just as much.

Since both Koufax and Ford had made only one mistake in the tense struggle, the game entered the bottom of the seventh knotted at one all. The bright sun and clear blue sky, which was a California trademark, would now contribute to the turning point of the game.

Fleet-footed Junior Gilliam led off the inning with a high chopper down the third-base line. Boyer fielded the ball and rifled his throw to first. The first-baseman, a normally sure-handed Joe Pepitone, lost the ball in the glare of the sun and a sea of light-colored shirts in the background. The ball traveled into right field, as Gilliam, running like a frightened deer, raced all the way to third on the error.

Willie Davis, the next batter, lofted a fly ball into center field. Gilliam tagged up, and Mantle made a valiant effort to cut down the runner. He made a strong throw to the plate, but Gilliam barely beat Howard's tag to score the go-ahead run.

This being the era of nine-inning pitchers, Sandy Koufax was not only baseball's best starting pitcher, but its best closer as well. Given the lead late in the game, the Dodgers would not let this one get away. When Hector Lopez, who was filling in for the injured Roger Maris in right field, sent a soft grounder to Maury Wills at short, the Series was over. The formerly invincible New York Yankees, who were victims of some of the greatest pitching in World Series history, had been swept in four straight.

Even though the four games were all tight, hard-fought contests, the New Yorkers never had a chance. The Dodger staff posted a 1.00 earned-run average and completely shut down the Yankee hitters.

The Hollywood club had now won their third straight World Championship under manager Walter Alston. The '55 triumph in Brooklyn, their only Series triumph in the New York borough, preceded two consecutive victories in Los Angeles.

In the early and mid Sixties, Sandy Koufax was baseball's dominant left-handed pitcher. He was nearly unhittable with excellent control; a marvel on the mound.

The losing pitcher, Whitey Ford, actually pitched a better game than Koufax. While Sandy gave up six hits, Ford limited LA to two safeties in his seven innings of work. He made only one bad pitch, which Frank Howard took deep, and an unfortunate error decided the final outcome.

The Dodgers joined the Boston Braves, New York Giants, and of course the Yankees as teams that swept their opponents in four games. The '63 World Series was the first one in which the Yanks suffered a whitewash. In 1922 the Giants defeated them by a 4-0 margin, but one game ended tied, when it was called by darkness during the era before stadium lights.

The defeat was especially bitter for Yankee skipper Ralph Houk. Houk had won the World Series in his first two seasons as manager. He was firmly convinced that he still had baseball's best team, so finishing as a runner-up was hard to swallow. While Houk still may have had the top club in the game, his squad had the misfortune of running into Koufax, Drysdale, and Podres at the peak of their careers.

DODGERS-YANKEES RECAP

	R	H	E
Dodgers	2	2	1
Yankees	1	6	1

Winning pitcher- Koufax
Losing pitcher- Ford
Home runs- F. Howard, Mantle

HEROES ** F. Howard, Koufax
GOAT < Pepitone

1964

MAJOR HEADLINES

The Peoples' Republic of China detonates its first atomic bomb.

The Medicare government health insurance program for people over sixty-five is established.

Congress passes the Tonkin Gulf Resolution authorizing presidential action in Vietnam after the North Vietnamese attack two naval destroyers.

The Warren Commission releases its report that Lee Harvey Oswald acted alone in the assassination of President Kennedy.

Lyndon Johnson trounces Barry Goldwater in the presidential election.

SPORTS

Baseball- St. Louis Cardinals edge the NY Yankees in a seven-game World Series.

Pro Football- Cleveland wins the NFL Title by shutting out Baltimore.

College Football- Alabama is voted the National Champion.

Pro Basketball- Boston defeats the San Francisco Warriors in the NBA finals.

College Basketball- UCLA wins the NCAA Championship from Duke in the final.

Hockey- Toronto takes third straight Stanley Cup by beating Detroit.

U.S. Open Tennis-
    Men's Finals: Roy Emerson defeats Fred Stolle.
    Women's Finals: Maria Bueno defeats Carole Graebner.

MOVIES- ADADEMY AWARDS

Best Actor: Rex Harrison, *My Fair Lady*
Best Actress: Julie Andrews, *Mary Poppins*
Best Director: George Cukor, *My Fair Lady*
Best Picture: *My Fair Lady*

CHAPTER XIX
A BATTERY ASSAULT

Monday, October 12, 1964- Yankee Stadium, Bronx, NY
World Series Game Five, St. Louis Cardinals 5, New York Yankees 2
(10 innings)

As traditional hosts, the New York Yankees welcomed the St. Louis Cardinals back to the World Series in 1964. The Bronx Bombers were making their fifth straight appearance in the Fall Classic, but the Cards were making their first postseason appearance in eighteen years. Neither team had an easy path to the October Games, as both clubs won the pennant on the final day of the season.

After splitting two routine affairs in St. Louis, the third and fourth games in New York each featured dramatic game-winning home runs. Mickey Mantle won Game Three with a ninth-inning blast, and the Cardinals' all-star third-baseman, Ken Boyer, walloped a grand slammer to wipe out a three-run Yankee lead and even the Series at two apiece.

A critical fifth game thus loomed. The fans were still buzzing about the sudden heroics of the last two matches, but, as the great jazz singer, Al Jolson, might have exclaimed, "You aint' seen nuthin yet!"

The fifth game at Yankee Stadium promised to be another tense struggle. The Cards' fireballing right-hander, Bob Gibson, and the Yankees' outstanding rookie, Mel Stottlemyre, who was their best pitcher in the last half of the season, were the mound opponents in this battle. The Yanks had fallen into third place during the summer, and without the young sinker-ball specialist, most likely would have settled into their winter homes by now.

Both hurlers appeared vigorous, but some shoddy fielding by the New Yorkers in the Cardinal fifth and a disputed umpiring decision cost the Yanks the only two runs scored entering the ninth inning.

Gibson led off the fifth frame with a bloop hit that fell in between shortstop Phil Linz and left-fielder Tom Tresh, as both had their signals crossed on who would catch the ball. Stottlemyre wanted ground balls, and ground balls he got.

The plan didn't work as expected. Richardson booted a perfect double-play ball at second, and Lou Brock's grounder, as if directed by radar, found a hole into right field for the first run.

Bill White then hit another grounder to Richardson that he fielded cleanly this time. He tossed to Linz, who fired to first for what looked like an inning-ending double-play. Umpire Al Smith didn't see it that way though. Despite heavy protests from the New York side, he ruled that the first-baseman had beaten the relay, and the Red Birds had their second run.

With a defiant Bob Gibson still brushing back batters from the plate as the Yankees took their ninth turn at bat, it looked like an imposing shutout for the big right-hander. But as manager Yogi Berra once said, "It aint' over till it's over." Since a costly Yankee error gave St. Louis a run, it only seemed fitting that the Cards return the favor for their hosts.

Card shortstop Dick Groat bobbled an easy grounder, and Mantle was safe at first. Both Richardson and Groat were usually sure-handed, and their defense contributed mightily to the success of their respective teams. Even so, errors are part of the game, and after retiring the next two batters, Gibson still had to get one more to close out the day's business.

The last hope of the Yankees was Tom Tresh. As the disappointed crowd started to head for the exits to beat the congested Bronx rush-hour traffic, Tresh belted a long drive to right-center field. The mammoth blast sailed into the distant bleachers, and suddenly the crowd found its way back to their seats as the game continued. The homer forced the tired athletes to put in for overtime on this long afternoon.

Bill White was a patient hitter, and the first-baseman led off the Cardinal tenth with a walk. With Boyer at the plate, the fearful crowd remembered the slugger's homerun that cleaned the bases and won the previous game. Boyer though surprised both the crowd and the Yankees as he beat out a perfectly-executed bunt between the mound and first base.

With one out, Tim McCarver, Gibson's battery mate, and the World Series' leading hitter, strode to the plate. Reliever Peter Mikkelsen, like Stottlemyre, threw a good sinker. After drawing a full count on the catcher, Mikkelsen didn't want to walk him. He delivered a pitch too high up in the zone, and McCarver drilled it deep to right. The ball landed in the seats for a three-run dinger.

Gibson retired the Yanks in the tenth to gain a triumph that put the Red Birds, like Hertz, in the driver's seat. His strikeout total of thirteen was the third highest in World Series history, only exceeded by Sandy Koufax with fifteen and Carl Erskine with fourteen. If Sandy Koufax was the dominant left-handed pitcher in the Sixties, then Bob Gibson was certainly the dominant right-hander of the decade. He would return with only two days rest to hurl yet another complete-game victory in the seventh and deciding contest to bring the World Championship to St. Louis.

The great Yankee catcher, Yogi Berra, had completed his brilliant playing career and led the Bronx Bombers to the World Series in his first year as their manager. He came close to duplicating the accomplishments of his predecessors, Casey Stengel and Ralph Houk, both of whom won the World Series in their first year at the helm. It took a stubborn and determined St. Louis Cardinal baseball squad to foil Yogi in his victory quest by the length of a cigar. The fifth game was as exciting and dramatic as a World Series game could be, and it proved to be the highlight of the season for St. Louis.

As late as August 14, the Red Birds appeared to be going nowhere but home at the end of the season. They were fourth in the standings, eleven and a half games out of first. Their manager, Johnny Keane, was about to be fired.

From that point they surged to the top, clinching the pennant on the final day of the season. The Cardinals' outstanding battery of Gibson and McCarver contributed heavily to the surge, winning nine out of ten games in September. The battery assault on the Yankees in Game Five was the turning point in one of the most remarkable comebacks in baseball history, which lifted the St. Louis Cardinals from oblivion to the top of the baseball world.

CARDINALS-YANKEES RECAP

	R	H	E
Cardinals	5	10	1
Yankees	2	6	2

Winning pitcher- Gibson
Losing pitcher- Mikkelsen
Home runs- Tresh, McCarver

HEROES ** Gibson, McCarver
GOAT < Mikkelsen

1965

MAJOR HEADLINES

President Johnson authorizes continued bombing of North Vietnam.

Black civil rights leader Malcolm X is assassinated.

Martin Luther King leads a march from Selma, AL to Montgomery to demonstrate for more voting rights for Southern blacks.

Civil rioting in the Watts section of Los Angeles results in thirty-four deaths and $200 Million of property damages.

A massive electric power failure blacks out much of the Northeastern United States and two Canadian provinces.

SPORTS

Baseball- LA Dodgers defeat the Minnesota Twins in seven games in the World Series.

Pro Football- Green Bay defeats Cleveland for the NFL title.

College Football- Alabama and Michigan State share the National Championship.

Pro Basketball- The Celtics whip the Lakers in the NBA finals.

College Basketball- UCLA beats Michigan in the NCAA final.

Hockey- Montreal defeats Chicago to win the Stanley Cup.

U.S. Open Tennis-
    Men's Finals: Manuel Santana defeats Cliff Drysdale.
    Women's Finals: Margaret Smith defeats Billie Jean Moffitt.

MOVIES- ACADEMY AWARDS

Best Actor: Lee Marvin, *Cat Ballou*
Best Actress: Julie Christie, *Darling*
Best Director: Robert Wise, *The Sound of Music*
Best Picture: *The Sound of Music*

CHAPTER XX
SANDY'S A DANDY

Thursday, October 14, 1965- Metropolitan Stadium, Bloomington, MN
World Series Game Seven, Los Angeles Dodgers 2, Minnesota Twins 0

Would it be Drysdale or Koufax? That was the big question before the seventh and final game of the 1965 World Series at Metropolitan Stadium in Bloomington, Minnesota. Once again, the Los Angeles Dodgers, on the strength of superlative pitching and speed, were making their second World Series appearance in three years.

After their four-game sweep of the Yankees in '63, Los Angeles had an off-year in 1964 due to multiple injuries at key positions. Nevertheless, with Sandy Koufax and Don Drysdale filling half the pitching rotation, that mound prowess would cover up flaws on any team.

The New York Yankees, like the Dodgers in 1964, had an off-season in '65. The Yanks failed to show up for postseason play for only the third time in the past seventeen years

The Minnesota Twins replaced them and became the American League representatives. The club that floundered in Washington as the Senators finally abandoned the Nation's Capital. They now flourished in the Minneapolis-St. Paul area of Minnesota, were renamed the Twins, and became an up-and-coming power in the Junior Circuit. The Twins outdistanced the rest of the AL competition with ease and brought the first pennant to the Twin Cities.

The normal Dodger rotation consisted of Koufax, Drysdale, and an outstanding acquisition, southpaw Claude Osteen. The problem was that the opening day of the World Series was also Yom Kippur, the holiest day in the Jewish calendar. Observing the holiday, Koufax was not in uniform for the opener. So manager Walter Alston gave the ball to Don Drysdale, a pretty fair substitute.

After six games, the World Series was even, with each team having won all of its home games. Although it was Drysdale's turn to hurl the deciding game, some speculation arose that Koufax would be Alston's choice to start the seventh game with only two days rest, as Bob Gibson had done in the previous Series.

Koufax had shutout the Twins impressively in his last start in Game Five. Alston's decision was one that every other major league manager envied. He finally decided that Koufax would start, and Drysdale would be warming up in the bullpen, ready to take over, should Koufax tire or need some help. The Dodgers thus had their Number One starter and Number One-A ready to go against the powerful Minnesota lineup. Opposing the West Coast club would be the Twins' formidable lefthander, Jim Katt.

In the very first inning, it appeared that Koufax might not have been ready to assume the burden. His control wasn't as sharp as usual, and he walked two dangerous batters, Tony Oliva and Harmon Killibrew. Rising to the occasion, Sandy struck out catcher Earl Battey to snuff out the budding rally.

The Dodgers believed that the least they could do for their pitching icon was to get him some runs to work with. That way either Koufax or Drysdale would slam the door shut as they had done so many times during the regular campaign.

In the visitors' fourth, left-fielder Lou Johnson greeted Katt with a home run to left. Johnson, although often unappreciated, never had a more important hit in his career. A Ron Fairly double and a Wes Parker single quickly followed, and LA had a pair of runs. A two-run cushion against the heavy-hitting Twins would normally be nothing significant, but facing one and possible two mound legends was like trying to climb Mount Everest.

Though he was shaky in the early innings, Koufax managed to stay out of trouble. He had one more tough inning, the fifth. A double and a walk put the tying runs on base with only one out. It was here that a fielding gem by third-sacker Junior Gilliam shielded the pitching star from further harm.

Shortstop Zoilo Versalles, who was to become the American League's Most Valuable Player, smacked a hard grounder down the third-base line. Gilliam smartly backhanded the ball and stepped on the bag for the force. An easy ground out then ended the inning without any damage.

From the fifth inning on, Koufax appeared to get stronger. Don Drysdale's chances of appearing in the game were diminishing with every pitch.

The Angelinos had several more scoring opportunities but couldn't capitalize on them. As the contest entered the home ninth, Koufax was still firing away.

When Killebrew lined a hard single to left with one out, the potential tying run came to the plate. The unflinching but fatigued southpaw then reached back with his last ounce of strength. He struck out the final two batters, Batty and Bob Allison, then walked off the mound, both elated and relieved that the World Series was over. The LA Dodgers were World Champions for the third time in their eight years in California.

After his unsettled start, Sandy Koufax calmed down to hurl his second impressive win in three days. The writers' decision to designate him the outstanding player of the 1965 World Series was a no-brainer. His stats for the day included allowing only three hits, walking three, and striking out ten. These accomplishments would thrill most pitchers, but this was just another day at the office for the great lefty.

Koufax's game was a microcosm of his season. Despite developing an arthritic elbow that threatened his career, Sandy nevertheless won twenty-six games, set a season strikeout record, and hurled a perfect game.

Although Koufax and his fans didn't realize it at the time, his seventh-game shutout of Minnesota would be his last World Series victory. Sandy Koufax would have one more outstanding season, but the chronic elbow condition would force him to retire at the age of thirty-one. During his abbreviated but brilliant career, he was one of the greatest pitchers the game of baseball has ever seen.

DODGERS-TWINS RECAP

	R	H	E
Los Angeles	2	7	0
Minnesota	0	3	1

Winning pitcher- Koufax
Losing pitcher- Kaat
Home run- Johnson

HERO * Koufax
GOAT < None

1966

MAJOR HEADLINES

U.S. planes commence bombing of the North Vietnamese capital of Hanoi.

Air Force Major William Knight sets a world air speed record by flying 4233 miles per hour in an X-15 jet.

Indira Ghandi becomes Prime Minister of India.

Edward Brooke of Massachusetts is the first black man to be elected to the U.S. Senate since the Reconstruction era.

The Supreme Court outlaws poll taxes as a means for voter eligibility.

SPORTS

Baseball- Baltimore Orioles sweep the Los Angeles Dodgers in the World Series.

Pro Football- Green Bay edges Dallas in the NFL title game.

College Football- Notre Dame is voted the National Champion.

Pro Basketball- Boston defeats Los Angeles in the NBA championship.

College Basketball- Texas El Paso defeats Kentucky in the NCAA final.

Hockey- Montreal defeats Detroit in the Stanley Cup finals.

U.S. Open Tennis-
    Men's Finals: Fred Stolle beats John Newcombe.
    Women's Finals: Maria Bueno beats Nancy Richey.

MOVIES- ACADEMY AWARDS

Best Actor: Paul Schofield, *A Man for All Seasons*
Best Actress: Elizabeth Taylor, *Who's Afraid of Virginia Woolf?*
Best Director: Fred Zinneman, *A Man for All Seasons*
Best Picture: *A Man for All Seasons*

CHAPTER XXI
CATCH 22, DROP A FEW

Thursday, October 6, 1966- Dodger Stadium, Los Angeles, CA
World Series Game Two, Baltimore Orioles 6, Los Angeles Dodgers 0

For every hero that emerges in a sporting contest, there usually exists a goat to counter the heroics. This was the case in the second World Series game of 1966, played at the Dodgers' beautiful home in downtown Los Angeles, Dodger Stadium.

For the second straight year, the Dodgers, on the strength of superlative pitching, were the National League standard-bearers. For the second straight year, their American League opponents, now that the Yankees had become mere mortals, were a club that changed not only its home address, but also its identity.

In 1965 the Minnesota Twins, descendants of the lowly Washington Senators, represented the Junior Circuit, and now the Baltimore Orioles were attempting to put the losing image of the St. Louis Browns behind them. The offspring of those sad-sack Brownies now brought the first pennant to the shores of the Chesapeake Bay.

The formidable Birds had the American League Triple Crown winner in Frank Robinson, the magic glove of third-baseman Brooks Robinson, and the strong bat of lumbering slugger, Boog Powell, but the Californians were favored based on both their pitching and their postseason experience. So when the Orioles surprised the Dodgers by beating Don Drysdale in the opener, the second game became crucial to LA.

No team wants to lose its first two games at home, as this places them in an almost hopeless position from which to recover. The Dodgers asked, or maybe even begged their superman, Sandy Koufax, to win a vital encounter as he had so often done before.

The game looked like a mismatch, when Baltimore started its promising but inexperienced young right-hander, twenty-year-old Jim Palmer. The match remained scoreless through the first four innings, but when the Orioles came to bat in the fifth, the gremlins took over the field and made center-fielder Willie Davis their chief victim.

With one down and a man on first, Paul Blair lofted a fly ball to center. Looking into the glare of the afternoon sun, Davis flipped down the glasses but lost the ball at the last moment. It hit off his glove and struck the ground for a two-base error.

The Dodgers elected not to walk the next man to load the bases. They instead decided to bring in the infielders, hoping to cut off a run at the plate. So much for that strategy—the batter, Andy Etchebarren, hoisted another fly ball into short left-center. It was déjà vu all over again, as Davis camped under it but again lost sight of the ball at the last moment. It popped out of his glove, as the first run of the game crossed the plate.

This time Davis picked up the ball and fired toward third base, trying to cut down the speeding Blair. The ball sailed high over Junior Gilliam's head. Blair scored, and Etchebarren wound up at third.

Although the two runs were unearned, the unfortunate Koufax had yielded his first runs in his last twenty-three innings of World Series play. When the next batter, Luis Aparicio, singled, the Orioles had a three-run lead.

Curt Blefary mercifully lined out to end the horrid stanza. Davis wrote himself into the record book as the first World Series player to commit three errors in one inning.

The crowd rewarded him for his culpable performance with a derisive chorus of boos. For this the beleaguered outfielder tipped his cap in mock appreciation.

Since Gilliam had committed an error in the fourth inning, the Dodger miscue total was four and counting. The Hollywood club was playing like it had answered a casting call to appear in a Three Stooges movie.

In the Baltimore sixth, Davis and right-fielder Ron Fairly converged on a drive to right-center by Frank Robinson, but let it drop between them like it was contaminated. The official scorer reluctantly had no choice but to give Robinson a triple. Los Angeles would have to earn its errors. Powell followed with a single to make it 4-0.

The parade of errors continued after second-sacker Dave Johnson stroked another hit to right. Fairly tried to cut down Powell, who was streaking for third base. The throw bounced past Gilliam for error number five. The Dodgers averted further damage, but four innings still remained for them to tie or break the team record for errors in a World Series game.

The historic moment finally came in the Oriole eighth. The Birds had runners on second and third, when Johnson smacked an infield single off the pitcher's glove. Ron Perranoski, who had relieved Koufax, stumbled while attempting to field the elusive baseball. He flipped it toward first, but the ball sailed past a helpless Wes Parker, as two more runs scored.

The frustrated Angelinos failed to commit any more errors, so they had to settle for a share of the futility record with the Chicago White Sox of 1906 and 1917, and the 1909 Pittsburgh Pirates, who also bungled six fielding plays in a Series game.

The humiliating defeat set the stage for a four-game sweep. The Baltimore manager, Hank Bauer, was familiar enough with winning from his playing days with the Yankees.

Although nobody knew it at the time, this would be Sandy Koufax' final appearance on the mound, since he would retire at the end of the season. As sad as the finale was for the superstar, Koufax only allowed one earned run in his six innings of labor.

For winning pitcher Jim Palmer, the game showcased his talent before a national TV audience and became the springboard that launched his Hall-of-Fame career. At age twenty, his 6-0 triumph made him the youngest pitcher ever to hurl a shutout in the World Series.

Willie Davis would have to wear the goat horns. Davis was normally a highly competitive player, but picked the worst time to have a dreadful game, in front of the whole country.

If TV reporters like CBS' Warner Wolf, with his "Plays of the Month," (mostly comical) and NBC's Len Berman, whose "Spanning the World" highlights the humorous blunders and bloopers in the world of sports, were looking for material in 1966, they could have found enough in this contest to start a mini-series.

The popular quiz show, "Jeopardy," could have posted an answer, "Catch 22." The question would then be, "How many balls would the Dodger fielders catch if one hundred were hit to them?"

ORIOLES-DODGERS RECAP

	R	H	E
Baltimore	6	8	0
Los Angeles	0	4	6

Winning pitcher- Palmer
Losing pitcher- Koufax
Home runs- none

HERO * Palmer
GOAT < W. Davis

1967

MAJOR HEADLINES

Israel is victorious against an Arab attack in the six-day war in the Middle East.

Bloody rioting in Newark and Detroit causes death and heavy destruction of property.

Congress passes the 25th Amendment, which allows the vice president to assume power if the president is incapacitated, and for the president to appoint a vice president if the post is vacant.

Thurgood Marshall is sworn in as the first black Supreme Court Justice.

Muhammad Ali is stripped of his Heavyweight boxing title for refusing to serve in the Armed Forces.

SPORTS

Baseball- St. Louis defeats Boston in seven-game World Series.

Pro Football- Green Bay trounces Kansas City Chiefs in the first Super Bowl. ('66 season)

College Football- Southern California is voted the National Champion.

Pro Basketball- Philadelphia 76ers beat San Francisco Warriors for the NBA championship.

College Basketball- UCLA defeats Dayton in the NCAA final.

Hockey- Montreal again defeats Detroit in the Stanley cup finals.

U.S. Open Tennis-
  Men's Finals: John Newcombe beats Clark Graebner.
  Women's Finals: Billy Jean King beats Ann Haydon Jones.

MOVIES- ACADEMY AWARDS

Best Actor: Rod Steiger, *In the Heat of the Night*
Best Actress: Katherine Hepburn, *Guess Who's Coming to Dinner*
Best Director: Mike Nichols, *The Graduate*
Best Picture: *In the Heat of the Night*

CHAPTER XXII
WEEKEND AT YASTRZEMSKI'S

Sunday, October 1, 1967- Fenway Park, Boston, MA
Final Sunday, Boston Red Sox 5, Minnesota Twins 3

The final game of the 1967 season was a baseball fan's dream. The two clubs in a flatfooted tie for first place prepared to square off to decide the American League pennant.

The participants in this winner-take-all feast were the Minnesota Twins and a surprising entry, the Boston Red Sox. The Twins had become a power in the Junior Circuit, while the Red Sox, who had usually fallen a buck short chasing the Yankees in the Forties and Fifties, spent most of the Sixties in the league's second division.

After a dismal ninth-place finish in 1966, the Sox employed a youth movement plus the magic talents of Ted Williams' successor in left field, Carl Yastrzemski, to remain in contention for the flag throughout the entire season. They trailed the Twins by one game as the clubs began their showdown two-game series at Fenway Park on the final weekend of the campaign.

Boston prevailed on Saturday, forcing the season into sudden death on Sunday. The evenly-matched adversaries both had freshman managers, Cal Ermer for Minnesota, and Dick Williams for the Bosox. Both pilots had twenty-game winners, Dean Chance for the Twins, and Jim Lonborg for the Red Sox, ready to start. Both managers too had squads with long-ball hitting to spare.

Each pitcher appeared to be sharp early in the contest, and it looked like runs would be hard to come by on this overcast afternoon in Boston.

The Twins staked Chance to an early lead with single markers in the first and third frames, but they didn't exactly overpower Lonborg. Slugger Harmon Killebrew drove in one run with a single, and first-baseman George Scott committed a throwing error allowing the second run to score.

Chance guarded his tenuous 2-0 lead into the home sixth, but Yastrzemski was just warming up. Hurler Lonborg started the Boston tee-off party with a bunt single. Two more hits loaded the bases, setting the table for the gifted Red Sox star.

Yaz had four hits, including a homer, in the previous-game victory. He had already banged out a single and double in this encounter, and a streak of four straight safeties in the two games. With his streak on the line as well as the game and the pennant, Carl stroked number five, a line single to center field. The hit drove in a pair and deadlocked the game. Although the Bosox could pound the friendly left-field wall known as the "Green Monster," the single by Yastrzemski was the biggest hit in Boston since *My Fair Lady*.

Yaz' hit was the catalyst that sparked the pennant-winning rally. Before the inning concluded, the delirious Boston fans witnessed four hits, one walk, a runner safe on a fielder's choice play, two wild pitches, and five runs crossing home plate.

Yastsrzemski finished off his sensational weekend with his sixth consecutive hit in the eighth inning, but he also made a key defensive play in the top half of the inning. With a run in and the Twins threatening, Yaz retrieved a hard-hit ball in the tricky left field corner and made a perfect throw to second base to cut down the runner. Instead of having a man on second and a run in, the throw snuffed out the attempted comeback by turning an attempted double into the third out.

The sensational play was the final nail in the coffin for Minny. Jim Lonborg's twenty-second victory, a 5-3 seven-hitter, was the icing on the cake in a Cy Young season for the young right-hander.

Carl Yastrzemski had a year in 1967 that most hitters could only dream of. He captured baseball's Triple Crown in the American League, leading in batting average, homeruns, and runs batted in. None were more important than numbers 120 and 121, which initiated the Boston tee-off party.

Yastrzemski finished the weekend with seven hits in eight at-bats. He preserved the final victory with his defensive gem and played the two weekend games like he played the entire season. Yaz would become the unanimous choice of the baseball writers as Most Valuable Player in the American League.

Most important, the Boston Red Sox pole-vaulted from ninth place to first, winning their first pennant in twenty-one years. They won it in front of their impassioned fans, and for once they didn't blow a game they needed to win.

RED SOX-TWINS RECAP

	R	H	E
Boston	5	12	2
Minnesota	3	7	1

Winning pitcher- Lonborg
Losing pitcher- Chance

HEROES ** Yastrzemski, Lonborg
GOAT < Chance

1968

MAJOR HEADLINES

Senator Robert F. Kennedy and black civil rights leader Martin Luther King are both gunned down by assassins' bullets.

Radical anti-war demonstrations are held on college campuses across the nation, forcing the cancellation of many graduation ceremonies.

Pan Am launches the first direct air service between the US and the Soviet Union.

President Johnson curbs the bombing of North Vietnam, and peace talks are started in Paris.

Police use violence in attempting to contain anti-war protestors outside the building holding the Democratic Convention in Chicago.

When President Johnson declines to seek re-election, Vice President Hubert Humphrey is picked to run for president.

Shirley Chisholm of New York is the first black woman elected to Congress.

Richard Nixon defeats Hubert Humphrey in the presidential election.

SPORTS

Baseball- Detroit Tigers edge the St. Louis Cardinals in seven games in the World Series.

Pro Football- Green Bay beats the Oakland Raiders in Super Bowl II. ('67 Seasons)

College Football- Ohio State is voted National Champion.

Pro Basketball- Boston defeats Los Angels for the NBA title.

College Basketball- UCLA beats North Carolina for the NCAA championship.

Hockey- Montreal defeats St. Louis in the Stanley Cup finals.

U.S. Open Tennis-
    Men's Finals: Arthur Ashe defeats Tom Okker.
    Women's Finals: Virginia Wade defeats Billy Jean King.

MOVIES- ACADEMY AWARDS

Best Actor: Cliff Robertson, *Charlie*
Best Actress: Katherine Hepburn, *The Lion in Winter*
                 Barbra Streisand, *Funny Girl* (Tie)
Best Director: Sir Carol Reed, *Oliver*
Best Picture: *Oliver*

CHAPTER XXIII
TURNING IT AROUND

Monday, October 7, 1968- Tiger Stadium, Detroit, MI
World Series Game Five- Detroit Tigers 5, St. Louis Cardinals 3

The St. Louis Cardinals of 1968 were attempting to become the first National League team to repeat as World Series winners since 1922, when the New York Giants last accomplished this feat. The defending champions had a three-to-one lead in games over their American League opponents, the Detroit Tigers. They were anxious to close out the Series, as the teams prepared for the fifth game at creaky old Tiger Stadium in Detroit.

The Tigers were making their first appearance in the Fall Classic since 1945. They had lost both games in the Motor City and didn't want to embarrass themselves by being blown away in front of their home fans.

When the Cardinals greeted lefty starter Mickey Lolich with three quick runs in the first inning, the fat lady started warming up her vocal chords. Before many of the sellout throng of 54,000 fans had settled into their seats, Lou Brock doubled, Curt Flood singled, and Orlando Cepeda, the former San Francisco Giant star, homered. Being down in games 3 to 1, and with St. Louis still taking batting practice in the first inning, it appeared that this was the end of the line for Detroit. If this was a boxing match, the referee would have contemplated stopping the bout.

Then a funny thing happened on the way to the trouncing. The Tigers decided that, as in the movie, *Network*, they were mad as hell and wouldn't take it anymore. They pushed across two runs in their half of the fourth frame on three hits, two of which were triples. The game was becoming an extra-base hit barrage.

The best, however, was yet to come for the Motowners. Lou Brock led off the visitors' fifth with his second double, a resounding smack off the left-field wall. The stellar outfielder was having his third outstanding World Series in as many appearances.

When Julian Javier singled to left, the man who was to set an all-time stolen-base record was on his way home with a vital insurance run.

Left-fielder Willie Horton then rifled a perfect throw to the plate. Brock collided with catcher Bill Freehan, but Freehan held on to the ball. The home-plate umpire signaled "out."

The Cards argued vehemently. They felt it wasn't humanly possible for Brock not to score from second on an outfield hit. The ump said that it was, and if they didn't like it, they should tell it to Ripley.

The pendulum, although moving, had not yet completed its swing as the game continued. With one out in the home seventh, the Bengals still trailing by a run, and the pitcher due up, manager Mayo Smith surprised everyone as he allowed Lolich to hit. The hurler rewarded Smith's faith by stroking a single to center. One more hit and base-on-balls later, Detroit found itself with the bags loaded, two out, and long-time Tiger legend Al Kaline at the plate.

Kaline had finally earned a reward for his sixteen years of excellence by playing in his first World Series. On the third pitch, he lashed a hard single to center, driving in the go-aheads runs. Although Kaline would amass more than 3,000 hits in his spectacular career, none would be more gratifying than this one-base knock against the Red Birds.

First-baseman Norm Cash, who along with Kaline represented one of the most lethal batting combinations in the American League, provided the encore with another RBI single. The Detroiters now held a 5 to 3 lead.

The game was not a piece of cake for Lolich, who had pitched well enough to stay out of trouble after the initial stanza. The Cardinals threatened but couldn't dent the plate. When they batted in the eighth, St. Louis had a man on and two dangerous right-hand batters, Cepeda and Mike Shannon, due up.

This was a logical spot for Smith to bring in a right-handed closer, but the manager decided to stay with his lefty starter. Lolich didn't disappoint him either, retiring the pair on a fly ball and a strike out.

In the ninth, the persistent Cardinal pilot, Red Schoendienst, sent up three pinch hitters to try to regain the lead. Two managed to hit safely, and the skipper sent Roger Maris up to bat.

The former Yankee immortal, the man who had broken Babe Ruth's single-season homerun record, was finishing his outstanding career in a St. Louis uniform. Although he represented the potential go-ahead run, Maris struck out.

The last hope of the Red Birds was the pesky Brock, the one man the Tigers would hate to see on base. The gritty Lolich induced Brock to tap back to the mound to end the game.

The Cardinals did not win another game, as the Tigers went back to St. Louis and decisively took the last two matches from their stunned rivals. Lolich, with only two days of rest, shut out the Cards and Bob Gibson in the deciding seventh game, for his third victory of the Series. The three World Series triumphs would earn him the series MVP award.

Detroit turned the fifth game, and eventually the whole World Series around on two heroic plays, Horton's perfect throw home, and Kaline's clutch game-winning hit. The Tigers upset the favored Cardinals using the momentum of these plays in the most dramatic game of the '68 World Series. Besides being the turning point of the October Classic, Game Five was the only one where the issue was in doubt until the final out.

TIGERS-CARDINALS RECAP

	R	H	E
Detroit	5	9	1
St. Louis	3	9	0

Winning pitcher- Lolich
Losing pitcher- Hoerner
Home run- Cepeda

HEROES *** Horton, Kaline, Lolich
GOAT < Brock

1969

MAJOR HEADLINES

U.S. Astronauts Neil Armstrong, Edwin Aldrin, and Michael Collins land their spacecraft, Apollo 11, on the moon. Armstrong and Aldrin become the first men ever to walk on the surface of the moon.

More than 500,000 people attend the Woodstock Music Festival in Bethel, NY. The crowd mainly consists of hippies, "peaceniks," and strong anti-war protestors.

The Mylai Massacre, in which hundreds of South Vietnamese civilians were killed in 1968, is made public.

President Nixon signs a major tax reform law, which will reduce or eliminate taxes of low-income families.

Senator Ted Kennedy pleads guilty to a misdemeanor, "Leaving the Scene of an Accident," in the Mary Jo Kopechne drowning on Chappaqueddick Island, MA.

SPORTS

Baseball- New York Mets surprise the Baltimore Orioles in winning the World Series.

Pro Football- New York Jets upset the Baltimore Colts in Super Bowl III. ('68 Season)

College Football- Texas is voted the National Champion.

Pro Basketball- Boston edges Los Angeles for the NBA championship.

College Basketball- UCLA defeats Purdue for the NCAA title.

Hockey- Montreal repeats as Stanley cup champion by besting St. Louis.

U.S. Open Tennis-
    Men's Finals: Rod Laver beats Tony Roche.
    Women's Finals: Margaret Smith Court beats Nancy Richey.

MOVIES- ACADEMY AWARDS

Best Actor: John Wayne, *True Grit*
Best Actress: Maggie Smith, *The Prime of Miss Jean Brodie*
Best Director: John Schlessinger, *Midnight Cowboy*
Best Picture: *Midnight Cowboy*

CHAPTER XXIV
THE MOON AND THE MIRACLE METS

Thursday, October 16, 1969- Shea Stadium, Flushing, NY
World Series Game Five- New York Mets 5, Baltimore Orioles 3

When Neil Armstrong and Edwin Aldrin became the first men ever to walk on the surface of the moon in 1969, the world experienced one of the greatest miracles of all time. Now the New York Mets were attempting to perform a miracle of their own; win the world championship of baseball.

Since their first year of existence in 1962, the expansion Mets had been the doormats of the National League, the laughing stock of baseball. Now, in their eighth year, they not only became competitive, but found themselves in the World Series against the powerful Baltimore Orioles of the American League.

Led by pitchers Tom Seaver and Jerry Koosman, outfielders Tommie Agee and Cleon Jones, and their popular manager, Gil Hodges, the former Brooklyn Dodger favorite, the Flushing crew leaped from a ninth-place finish to win their first National League pennant. They overcame a nine-game lead the Chicago Cubs had held in August and won the Eastern Division title by eight lengths.

Since further expansion brought the total of clubs in each league to twelve, the leagues both split into two divisions. Although they had the best record in the National League, the Mets had to meet the Western Division winners, the Atlanta Braves, in a best three-of-five playoff before making it to the finals. They swept that series and immediately became huge underdogs against an awesome Baltimore Oriole team that won the Eastern Division of the American League by nineteen games and then trounced the Minnesota Twins in the League Championship Series.

The men from Queens lost the Series opener 4 to 1, with eventual Cy Young pitching ace Tom Seaver on the mound, but as they had done all season, this relentless group could be bent but not broken. New York won the next three games and now stood on the threshold of achieving one of the biggest upsets in sports history.

Hodges selected Koosman, his top southpaw, to try to put away the Orioles. Koos limited the Birds to two hits in winning a tight 2 to 1 second game. His opponent was another lefty, twenty-game winner Dave McNally, the losing hurler in that match.

The Mets didn't want to return to Baltimore to risk finishing the Series in front of a hostile crowd. They hoped to close out this affair before the home folks in their bright new Flushing home, Shea Stadium. The colorful stadium, built in 1964, was located adjacent to the site of the 1964-65 World's Fair. The round, symmetrical field had appeared to be no more than a carnival site housing the bumbling Mets for the past five years. But now a talented, young pitching staff had held the Orioles to two runs in their three wins. Nevertheless it seemed impossible that they could continue to hold off this group of bashers much longer.

In the third frame, Baltimore started to work on Koosman. Unlike most pitchers, McNally was not an automatic out. With a man on, he walloped a long home run over the left field fence. Two outs later, Frank Robinson, the all-everything outfielder, launched a rocket into the parking lot beyond the bullpen for the third run of the inning. It appeared that the Birds couldn't wait to fly back to Baltimore to take back the Series.

Koosman began to settle down, and the Metropolitans, who had received numerous breaks during this miracle season, picked up a big one when they batted in the sixth. Cleon Jones led off and took what appeared to be a low ball thrown into the dirt. Jones argued that the ball struck his foot, and Hodges came out of the dugout to back up his player in the heated argument. Gil picked up the ball and showed it to umpire Lou DiMuro. Remembering the similar incident with Nippy Jones in the 1957 World Series, DiMuro examined the scuff marks the shoe polish had caused and awarded first base to Cleon.

Naturally the volatile Oriole manager, Earl Weaver, rushed out of his dugout to protest. The umpires held their ground and threatened Weaver with ejection, a familiar experience, if he didn't leave the field and quiet down.

Next up was the brilliant mid-season acquisition, Donn Clendenon. The first-baseman promptly slammed a home run into the mezzanine, his third round-tripper of the Series, to reduce the Baltimore margin to a run.

The Mets were not finished in the miracle department. An inning later, light-hitting second-baseman Al Weis cleared the wall in left to tie up the game. Weis had hit only two home runs all year, but now had the biggest hit of his career.

After the third inning, Koosman had slammed the door on the mighty Orioles. The contest entered the New York half of the eighth still tied. Then destiny would finally take over. Jones doubled, and outfielder Ron Swoboda, who had a spectacular, diving, game-saving catch in Game Four, now stroked the game-winning hit. He lined a hard smash down the left-field line, just out of desperate reach of Don Buford for another two-bagger. The insurance run then scored as Powell booted a grounder at first base and threw wildly past relief pitcher Eddie Watt, who tried to cover the bag.

The animated crowd readied themselves for an unbelievable celebration. Frank Robinson delayed the party by drawing a ninth-inning walk, but, with two out, Davey Johnson, who would ironically become the Mets' most successful manager after he finished his playing career, lofted a fly ball to deep left field. For what appeared to be an eternity, Jones waited for it to come down, squeezed it, and then dropped to one knee, before racing for the safety of the dugout. Against all odds, the New York Metropolitans were the World Champions of baseball.

Jerry Koosman settled down after his rough third inning to limit the Birds to one hit over the final six frames. He finished with a five-hitter, defeating the Orioles 5 to 3.

The fact that the Mets defeated the formerly invincible Baltimore Oriole club was in itself a miracle. However, the manner in which they won these games was even more remarkable. When the World Series moved back to New York after the Mets evened the Series in Baltimore, Tommie Agee made two incredible catches in center field to save five runs in the third game, and a young pitching prospect named Nolan Ryan came out of the bullpen to strike out Paul Blair with the bases loaded to end the game.

In Game Four, Swoboda made his scintillating grab, and star hurler Tom Seaver went the entire ten innings for the victory.

In the fifth and final game, the Mets received a second straight masterful effort from Koosman, and long-ball clutch hitting from Weis, a least-likely source.

Donn Clendenon's homer gave him three for the five-games. His impressive hitting against a formidable Oriole staff earned him the Series MVP award.

Neil Armstrong and Edwin Aldrin may have walked on the moon, but when Cleon Jones squeezed the ball in his glove for the final out of the game, the New York Mets were walking on a cloud.

METS-ORIOLES RECAP

	R	H	E
Mets	5	7	1
Orioles	3	5	2

Winning pitcher- Koosman
Losing pitcher- Watt
Home runs- McNally, F. Robinson, Clendenon, Weis

HEROES *** Weis, Swoboda, Koosman
GOATS << Powell, Watt

1970

MAJOR HEADLINES

National Guardsmen fire on anti-war protestors on the Kent State University campus in Ohio, killing four students.

A federal jury finds the "Chicago 7" anti-war activists innocent of conspiring to incite riots during the 1968 Democratic National Convention.

A postal reform measure creates the independent U.S. Postal Service.

SPORTS

Baseball- Baltimore overwhelms the Cincinnati Reds in five games in the World Series.

Pro Football- Kansas City upsets the Minnesota Vikings in Super Bowl IV. ('69 Season)

College Football- Nebraska and Texas share the National Title.

Pro Basketball- New York Knicks win their first NBA championship by beating the LA Lakers.

College Basketball- Perennial champion UCLA beats Jacksonville in the NCAA final.

Hockey- Boston Bruins beat the St. Louis Blues in the Stanley Cup finals.

U.S. Open Tennis-
    Men's Finals: Ken Rosewall beats Tony Roche
    Women's Finals: Margaret Smith Court beats Rosemary Casals.

MOVIES- ACADEMY AWARDS

Best Actor: George C. Scott, *Patton*
Best Actress: Glenda Jackson, *Women in Love*
Best Director: Franklin Schaffner, *Patton*
Best Picture: *Patton*

CHAPTER XXV
REVENGE OF THE BIRDS

Sunday, October 11, 1970- Riverfront Stadium, Cincinnati, OH
World Series Game Two- Baltimore Orioles 6, Cincinnati Reds 5

The National League pennant winner in 1970 was not to be envied. The Cincinnati Reds, under the leadership of manager Sparky Anderson, prepared to meet a very angry Baltimore Oriole squad that was still seething from its agonizing defeat at the hands of the New York Mets in 1969. The National League champs had to know that the Birds would unleash their wrath on their unfortunate opponents.

The '70 Series opened in the Reds' new home, Riverfront Stadium, appropriately named for its location on the banks of the Ohio River. For only the second time, the combatants would be playing on a field with artificial turf, where, unlike in the movies, it would be hard to follow the bouncing ball.

The Orioles were currently on a roll. They had a fifteen-game winning streak, closing out the regular campaign with eleven straight victories, adding three in the ALCS, plus a come-from-behind win in the Series opener.

In the first game, the O's had spotted Cincinnati a 3-0 lead but walloped three homers to take a 4-3 decision. Since no team had ever lost its first two games at home and come back to win a seven-game series, the situation was one of desperation for the Big Red Machine.

As in the opener, the Reds took the early lead, telling themselves and their fans that they would stay with the Orioles. Cincy tallied three times in the first at-bat, when Baltimore had difficulty adjusting to the carpeted field. Their usually rock-solid defense broke down, and they made two errors that helped lead to the scores.

The sure-handed shortstop, Mark Belanger, committed a rare miscue, bobbling a ground ball on the turf. Then Paul Blair, another defensive stalwart in center field, tried to backhand a Lee May double, which skipped past his glove, allowing a run to cross the plate.

Two innings later, when center-fielder Bob Tolan homered, the Orioles found themselves in a 4-0 hole. Baltimore southpaw Mike Cuellar was not looking like the twenty-four-game winner he was during the season. He then walked Johnnie Bench, the last batter he would face.

The Orioles would not fall any further behind, however. The Birds had a secret weapon at third base, Brooks Robinson. Lee May hit a scorcher down the line. It seemed like the hard-hitting first-baseman was always socking the ball in that direction, but Brooks sharply backhanded the ball and threw him out while on his knees to abort the rally. In this October Classic, Robinson displayed some of the most spectacular defense observers had ever seen at the hot corner.

Baltimore was not accustomed to trailing, so they started to mount a comeback. Boog Powell homered in the fourth to get one back. Then came the fifth, and the visitors made a statement that they would no longer tolerate a lead by the upstart Reds. Three straight singles opened the inning. Say goodbye to starter Jim McGlothin.

The reliever was a young twenty-year-old rookie, Milt Wilcox. The first batter he would have to face would be Powell, who was looking to pad his RBI total. The mammoth slugger slammed another single, as the Orioles pulled to within a run.

Brooks Robinson was not only having a sensational World Series with the glove, but a magnificent one with the bat as well. His sharp single to right tied the game.

The shell-shocked Reds had so far yielded five hard hits in a row. Catcher Eldrod Hendricks smacked the sixth, and it was the gamer. The lefty batter smashed a liner down the third-base line. Since Robinson was on his side, there was no one to grab the ball, and it went for a two-run double.

The five-run inning was an example of the cold efficiency with which the Baltimore club won many of its games all year long. Although the Red Machine was a credible opponent, this was not the Met pitching staff they were facing. No one else could suppress the lethal offense of this super team for very long.

All-star catcher Bench made it close, as he homered in the Cincinnati seventh, but the Oriole bullpen locked the door and threw away the key. Dick Hall, the forty-year old veteran, retired the last seven Reds to preserve the victory. The 6 to 5 triumph, the second straight Oriole road win, made the Reds' chances of winning extremely slim.

Baltimore secured the first two games in familiar fashion. They won both encounters by one run. Of the AL Champs' 108 season victories, they captured forty by a single run.

Brooks Robinson was brilliant both in the field and at the plate. He cleaned up everything his opponents hit in his direction so flawlessly that his fans wanted him to change his name to Hoover. The star's play made him the unanimous choice as World Series MVP, and led to a five-game stampede over their NL rivals.

After the humiliating defeat at the hands of the Mets the previous year, the revenge of the Birds was the fulfillment of a year-long quest to capture the World Series trophy. The Orioles always believed they were the best team on the planet, and now they were.

In the locker room following the second game, Powell summed up the feeling of his teammates with this prophetic comment, "We have a score to settle." The Cincinnati Reds got the message three games later.

ORIOLES-REDS RECAP

	R	H	E
Baltimore	6	10	2
Cincinnati	5	7	0

Winning pitcher- Phoebus
Losing pitcher- Wilcox
Home runs- Tolan, Powell, Bench
Save- Hall

HEROES ** Powell, Hall
GOATS << Mc Glothin, Wilcox

1971

MAJOR HEADLINES

First Lt. William Calley is found guilty in murdering twenty-two civilians in the My Lai Massacre of 1968.

The trade embargo against the Peoples' Republic of China is lifted.

The twenty-sixth Amendment giving eighteen-year olds the right to vote is passed in Congress.

Seven-thousand anti-war protestors are arrested in the Nation's Capital.

SPORTS

Baseball- Pittsburgh defeats Baltimore in seven games in the World Series.

Pro Football- Baltimore Colts edge the Dallas Cowboys in Super Bowl V. ('70 Season)

College Football- Nebraska wins the National Championship.

Pro Basketball- Milwaukee Bucks beat the Baltimore Bullets in the NBA finals.

College Basketball- UCLA keeps winning by beating Villanova in the NCAA final.

Hockey- Montreal over Chicago in Stanley Cup finals.

U.S. Open Tennis-
    Men's Finals: Stan Smith beats Jan Kodes.
    Women's Finals: Billie Jean King beats Rosemary Casals.

MOVIES- ACADEMY AWARDS

Best Actor: Gene Hackman, *The French Connection*
Best Actress: Jane Fonda, *Klute*
Best Director: William Friedkin, *The French Connection*
Best Picture: *The French Connection*

CHAPTER XXVI
THE SERIES GOES PRIME-TIME

Wednesday, October 13, 1971- Three Rivers Stadium, Pittsburgh, PA
World Series Game Four- Pittsburgh Pirates 4, Baltimore Orioles 3

A sixty-eight-year old baseball tradition was about to end. Since its inception in 1903, major league baseball always played World Series games in the afternoon. Now, a postseason contest was about to occur in the nighttime hours, so a much larger audience of working people could watch one of the games in the prime-time viewing hours and create a ratings bonanza for the NBC television network.

In addition to the usual sellout crowd, the network suits anticipated a record audience of sixty million people to tune in to the fourth game of the 1971 World Series at another in a rash of new National League ball parks, Three Rivers Stadium in Pittsburgh.

The recently-opened Pirate playpen received its name from its location at the junction of the Allegheny, Monongahela, and Ohio Rivers. It replaced the historic but outdated Forbes Field, which will always be remembered as the place where Bill Mazeroski struck the home run that won the 1960 World Series for the Pittsburghers. They were now returning to the October Classic for the first time since that monumental classic eleven years before.

The defending World Champion Baltimore Orioles had again shattered the competition in the American League and were holding a two-games-to-one advantage over the Bucs. They now hoped to impress the large television audience with a convincing arc-light victory and take one step closer to successfully defend their championship.

With this goal in mind, Baltimore went for the jugular right at the outset. They opened with three straight hits to load the bases for the dangerous clean-up batter, Frank Robinson.

The shaky Pittsburgh starter, Luke Walker, unleashed a wild pitch to score the Birds' first run. The Pirates then decided they didn't want to deal with Robby, so they gave him an intentional pass to reload the sacks.

The next two batters were the other Robinson, Brooks, and Powell. It was beginning to look like the Pirates would walk the plank. When each hitter belted a long fly out to the center field fence, two more runs scored, and manager Danny Murtaugh had seen enough of Walker for one night.

Murtaugh called upon a twenty-one-year old rookie, Bruce Kison, to stop the bleeding. Before he finished his ER shift, Kison would not only stop the bleeding, but he would wind up hurling six and a third innings of scoreless relief. Another rookie of the same age, Milt May, would deliver the game-winning hit in a rousing contest that provided an excellent debut for the World Series under the lights.

Kison's mission, which he gladly accepted, was to cool off the Orioles until the Pirate bats warmed up. This he did beyond all expectations.

Pittsburgh immediately got two markers back in their first at-bat. Hard-hitting Willie Stargell drove in the first with a long double into the right-center alley, scoring Dave Cash, who had walked.

The artificial turf of the new field even came to the aid of the home team. Al Oliver blooped a hit into center. When Paul Blair, the fine-fielding outfielder, tried for a shoe-string catch, the ball bounced high over his head like a Serena Williams slam and went for another run-scoring double.

The Pirate batters were definitely returning to life. In the home third, the great Roberto Clemente, one of baseball's best-kept secrets, was finally given a window to show the nation-wide fans what the people of Pittsburgh already knew- that he was one of the greatest players of his era. His two-out single kept a rally alive, and when Oliver again singled, the game was knotted.

Oriole starter Pat Dobson was one of four Baltimore hurlers who won at least twenty games. In this match, he was getting rocked, but pitched out of a bases-loaded jam in the fifth. He lasted through the sixth, and reliever Eddie Watt took the ball in the seventh stanza.

Watt wasn't much better than Dobson. He gave up three more hits, but when catcher Sanguillen overran second base and was out, Pittsburgh still had not dented the plate.

Kison had done a stellar job in relief, keeping Baltimore off the scoreboard since the rough first inning. His stint was up, however. With a runner on third and two out, it was time for one rookie to pinch hit for another. Milt May came off the bench to stroke a single to drive in the run that would decide the game.

The 4 to 3 Pirate victory was the keynote win in the World Series they would eventually capture in seven games. Roberto Clemente finally gained some of the recognition he had long deserved, as he earned the Most Valuable Player award in the '71 World Series.

The World Series night-game experiment was a success, as one of the largest TV audiences ever to watch a Series game tuned in to this one-run thriller.

The following year would see all weekday World Series affairs scheduled at night, and eventually baseball would completely phase out all Series games played in the daytime. The games to be played in late October nights would soon experience a cornucopia of weather conditions such as lengthy rain delays, blustery winds, sub-freezing temperatures, and even snow flurries.

The longer-lasting contests could sometimes end well past midnight. The World Series would become an insomniac's delight, especially in the Eastern time zone. Television would finally provide its late-night viewers with a week of escape from the mundane alternative of tuning in to the Psychic Hot Line, Home Shopping Network, or endless reruns of *I Love Lucy*.

PIRATES-ORIOLES RECAP

	R	H	E
Pittsburgh	4	14	0
Baltimore	3	4	1

Winning pitcher- Kison
Losing pitcher- Watt
Save- Giusti
Home runs- none

HEROES *** Kison, Guisti, May
GOATS << Dobson, Watt

1972

MAJOR HEADLINES

President Nixon pays an eight-day visit to China in what he calls, "A Journey of Peace."

The U.S. resumes bombing of Hanoi after a four-year halt, in response to North Vietnamese attacks across the demilitarized zone.

Alabama Governor George Wallace is shot and seriously wounded while campaigning for president at a suburban Maryland shopping center.

President Nixon becomes the first American president to visit Moscow for meetings with Kremlin leaders.

Five men are arrested for breaking into the Democratic National Committee headquarters in the Watergate complex in Washington, D.C.

Eleven Israeli athletes are murdered by Palestinian members of the Black September Group during the 1972 Summer Olympics in Munich.

President Nixon is reelected in a landslide victory over George McGovern.

SPORTS

Baseball: Oakland Athletics edge Cincinnati in seven-game World Series.

Pro Football- Dallas Cowboys trounce Miami Dolphins in Super Bowl VI. ('71 season)

College Football- Southern California is voted the National Champion.

Pro Basketball- Los Angeles defeats NY Knicks in the NBA Championship.

College Basketball- UCLA defeats Florida State in the NCAA Final.

Hockey: Boston Bruins beat NY Rangers in the Stanley Cup Finals.

U.S. Open Tennis-
    Men's Finals: Ilie Nastase beats Arthur Ashe
    Women's Finals: Billie Jean King defeats Kerry Melville.

MOVIES- ACADEMY AWARDS

Best Actor: Marlon Brando, *The Godfather*
Best Actress: Liza Minelli, *Cabaret*
Best Director: Bob Fosse, *Cabaret*
Best Picture: *The Godfather*

CHAPTER XXVII
A WILD MOOSE

Wednesday, October 11, 1972- Riverfront Stadium, Cincinnati, OH
National League Championship Series, Game Five,
Cincinnati Reds 4, Pittsburgh Pirates 3

Baseball championships have been decided in dramatic fashion, with homeruns, strikeouts, and spectacular catches, but never in such a bizarre manner as in the 1972 National League Championship Series. The Pittsburgh Pirates were determined to win another World Series. The defending World Champions, after dominating the NL Eastern Division, were now locked in a battle with their Western opponents, the Cincinnati Reds. With the playoff tied at two games apiece, the game that would decide the pennant was about to be contested at Riverfront Stadium in Cincinnati.

The start of the game was delayed an hour and a half by rain, prolonging the suspense. The hard-hitting Pirates had been leading two games to one, but could not win the clincher. The Reds decisively blew out the Bucs 7 to 1 in the fourth game to tie the series.

When the rain stopped, the Pittsburgh lumbermen started hitting. They tallied two runs in the second inning with three solid hits off Cincinnati's ace lefty, Don Gullett. After four it was 3 to 1. Pirate starter Steve Blass, who had shut out the Baltimore Orioles in the seventh game of the '71 World Series, was sailing along and looking stronger each inning.

As they had done throughout the NLCS, the Reds stayed within striking distance. Cesar Geronimo homered in the fifth to narrow the gap. The slumping outfielder had gone only one for seventeen in this series, so he picked a good time to show some life with the bat.

The Buc bullpen held Cincy into the ninth, and they needed just three outs to reenter the World Series. The Red Men took their final turn at bat with their season on the line.

Pittsburgh brought in their longtime relief ace, Dave Giusti, to wrap up a victory that would never come. Johnny Bench, the game's premiere catcher, and one of its premiere sluggers as well, promptly delivered a crushing home run to right to tie up the contest.

Bench only picked up where he left off during the season. His forty home runs and 125 runs batted in topped the majors in the 1972 season.

The next two batters, Tony Perez and Dennis Menke, both singled, and the winning run was in scoring position with nobody out. It was apparent that Giusti didn't have it today, so Bob Moose replaced him on the mound. Moose was one of Pittsburgh's regular starters, but Manager Danny Murtaugh asked him to go to the bullpen, where he was on call in this life-and-death struggle.

A fly ball to deep right advanced pinch-runner George Foster to third, so Cincinnati had runners at the corners with only one out. They could win the pennant with a fly ball or an infield out.

Darrel Chaney then popped a fly ball softly into left field, where the shortstop, Gene Alley, collided with the left-fielder, Rennie Stennett, but held on to the ball for the second out. Moose no longer had to worry about anything but retiring a batter to sent the battle into sudden death.

Death was more sudden to the Pirates, however, than they expected. With Hal McRae the batter, and a one-ball, one-strike count, Moose uncorked a wild pitch into the dirt. The ball struck the carpet, bounced over catcher Manny Sanguillen's head, and rolled to the backstop, as Foster trotted in with the pennant-winning run for the Red Men.

Moose had tried to induce McRae into swinging at a bad pitch, but let it get away from him, and the home crowd became ecstatic. Long-time Pirate fans recalled the 1927 World Series, in which hurler John Miljus tossed a wild pitch in the bottom of the ninth inning of the fourth game. That errant delivery enabled the Yankees to score the winning run and sweep the Series.

Since the League Championship Series format was initiated in 1969, the playoffs had been one-sided in both leagues. Thus 1972 was a breakthrough year, in that each championship playoff lasted a full five games, with the exciting Reds-Pirates battle and the Oakland Athletics outlasting the Detroit Tigers in the American League final.

The Bucs fielded a most impressive team during the regular season, with terrific hitting, great defense, adequate starting pitching, and a strong bullpen. They won ninety-six games during the season, but could not defend their World Championship crown. Pittsburgh never trailed in this Series, or in this game, until Bob Moose bounced a wild pitch, and bounced the Pirates out of the playoffs.

REDS-PIRATES RECAP

	R	H	E
Cincinnati	4	7	1
Pittsburgh	3	8	0

Winning pitcher- Carroll
Losing pitcher- Giusti
Home runs- Geronimo, Bench

HEROES ** Bench, Foster
GOATS << Giusti, Moose

1973

MAJOR HEADLINES

A cease-fire agreement to end the Vietnam War is reached in Paris.

The military draft is ended and replaced by an all-volunteer army.

Vice President Agnew is forced to resign after charges of income tax evasion. He is replaced by Gerald Ford, who is appointed under the new 25th amendment.

Several of President Nixon's top aides resign after charges of White House efforts to obstruct justice in the Watergate break-in.

The Supreme Court rules in the "Roe vs. Wade" case that abortions may be legal during the first three months of pregnancy.

Israel repels another attack by Egypt and Syria, started on the holiest day of the Jewish calendar, Yom Kippur.

SPORTS

Baseball- Oakland defeats the NY Mets in seven games in the World Series.

Pro Football- Miami finishes an undefeated season (1972) by downing the Washington Red Skins in Super Bowl VII. (1972 Season)

College Football- Alabama and Notre Dame share the National Championship.

Pro Basketball- NY Knicks beat the LA Lakers for the NBA title.

College Basketball- UCLA defeats Memphis State to win another NCAA championship.

Hockey- Montreal beats Chicago in the Stanley Cup finals.

U.S. Open Tennis-
    Men's Finals: John Newcombe defeats Jan Kodes.
    Women's Finals: Margaret Smith Court defeats Evonne Goolagong.

MOVIES- ACADEMY AWARDS

Best Actor: Jack Lemmon, *Save the Tiger*
Best Actress: Glenda Jackson, *A Touch of Class*
Best Director: George Roy Hill, *The Sting*
Best Picture: *The Sting*

CHAPTER XXVIII
CAN YOU BELIEVE IT?

Wednesday, October 10, 1973- Shea Stadium, Flushing, NY
National League Championship Series, Game Five
New York Mets 7, Cincinnati Reds 2

Followers of the New York Mets who had never believed they would see their favorite team play in a World Series were delirious with joy when the Mets won the 1969 World Series against the powerful Baltimore Orioles. The same skeptics were astounded, when the 1973 Metropolitans, who were in last place on Labor Day, vaulted to the top of the National League Eastern Division by season's end.

Although they survived a weak field in the East, the Flushing residents were given little chance of beating the strong Western Champion Cincinnati Reds. Yet here they were, tied at two games each with the Big Red Machine.

The magic number was only one. The New Yorkers merely had to win one game, and the team that had floundered through the Sixties would earn another appearance in its second World Series event in four years.

With their ace right-hander, Tom Seaver, taking the mound before the home folks at Shea Stadium, who was to say that the Mets wouldn't pull off another upset with the same magnitude as the '69 club?

The game started off as if it would become a wild free-for-all. Seaver pitched out of a bases-loaded jam, but Reds' starter Jack Billingham was not as fortunate. Ed Kranepool, the only Met player left over from the inept '62 club that lost 120 games, singled in a pair of runs to jump-start the team and the crowd.

Cincinnati retaliated with single markers in the third and fifth frames to force a stalemate. The season's climax awaited both squads, as the Mets prepared to bat in their half of the fifth inning.

Wayne Garrett, the steady third-baseman, was not having a good series. Garrett was hitless in his last nineteen at-bats. He now broke the spell with a leadoff double into the right-center-field gap. Garrett's counterpart at third, Dan Driessen, then committed a mental error, which proved costly. Felix Millan, the sparkplug second-baseman, bunted. Driessen fielded the bunt and touched third base, but failed to tag Garret. Since there was no automatic force, both runners were safe, and the rowdy Shea crowd, like a school of sharks, started to smell blood.

Cleon Jones, one of the Flushing crew's most dependable hitters, then smacked a double off the left-field wall, for what would become the pennant-winning hit.

The veteran Red manager, Sparky Anderson, saw that a good lefty hitter, John Milner, was due up, so he brought in his top left-handed starter, Don Gullett, from the pen. This time the strategy failed, as Milner drew a pass to load the sacks.

Met manager Yogi Berra was not about to be upstaged by Sparky. Although the left-hitting Kranepool had driven in the New Yorkers' first two runs, Yogi searched for a capable righty bat to come off the bench and wrap up the game. After winning a pennant in the Bronx, he was now determined to win another one in the borough of Queens to cover forty percent of the city.

As Berra scanned the bench, who just happened to be sitting on the pines but a forty-two-year old veteran named Willie Mays. The former Giant legend, who began playing in the Polo Grounds, had returned to New York to finish his magnificent career with the Mets. Willie was batting for the first time in a month, since cracking three ribs in a game in Montreal.

Mays has swatted many more powerful hits than the one he was about to strike, but none more significant. Willie hit a chopper in the dirt that bounced high in the air towards third base. By the time the ball came down, Millan had scored, and Mays had his first hit since the end of August. With Kranepool and Mays contributing to the attack, it was turning out to be Nostalgia Day at the Big Shea.

Outfielder Don Hahn made it 5 to 2 with another safety, and it was beginning to appear that there would be more baseball at the Flushing ballpark the following week. The noise level was deafening.

The diminutive shortstop, Bud Harrelson, who had been involved in a brawl with the brawny Red star, Pete Rose, the previous afternoon, followed with still another single to drive in the fourth run of the inning. Then in the following frame, Seaver wanted to show everyone that he could hit as well as pitch. So he walloped a long double and scored on another hit by the omnipresent Cleon Jones.

The Mets were now in great shape. They had a five-run lead with only three innings to go.

The crowd, however, was getting too involved in the action. They did what Cincinnati couldn't do- they stopped the Mets. As the ninth inning began, hordes of over-zealous fans stormed onto the field, reaching for sod, fixtures, and whatever else they could get their hands on. This reckless action stopped the game until order could be restored. These short-sighted hoodlums failed to realize that the World Series would require the use of the field for two or three more games the following week.

After about a thirty-minute delay, play finally resumed, and the Reds were not yet roasted. They loaded the bases with only one out. Yogi removed Seaver and had him escorted to the safety of the Met clubhouse.

He then summoned his top reliever, Tug McGraw. McGraw did his thing and retired the last two batters to preserve the victory for Seaver.

The Mets spent most of the summer in the NL East cellar. As the month of September rolled around, they started to win. McGraw kept repeating his reassuring phrase, "You Gotta Believe," the southpaw closer kept coming out of the bullpen to save his tiring starters, and the Mets and their fans finally started to believe.

The club won twenty out of their final twenty-six games to march to their second NL East flag. Within one month, they went from worst to first, then took the heavily favored Cincinnati Reds in an emotional five-game playoff to make it to their second World Series. Can you believe it?

METS-REDS RECAP

	R	H	E
NY Mets	7	13	1
Cincinnati	2	7	1

Winning pitcher- Seaver
Losing pitcher- Billingham
Home runs- none

HEROES ** Seaver, Jones
GOATS << Billingham, Driessen

1974

MAJOR HEADLINES

The House Judiciary Committee votes to recommend three articles of impeachment against President Nixon in the Watergate cover-up.

Under the threat of impeachment, President Nixon resigns from office. Vice President Gerald Ford assumes the office as his successor.

A prolonged oil embargo by Arab countries causes fuel prices to soar and long lines to form at gas stations around the nation.

President Ford announces an unconditional pardon for any Federal crimes committed by Former President Nixon while he was in office.

Patty Hearst, daughter of millionaire publisher Randolph Hearst, is abducted by Symbionese Liberation militants.

Atlanta Braves slugger Hank Aaron belts his 715th career home run to break Babe Ruth's record.

SPORTS

Baseball: Oakland wins its third straight World Series by defeating Los Angeles.

Pro Football: Miami beats Minnesota in Super Bowl VIII. ('73 Season)

College Football: Oklahoma and Southern California share the National Title.

Pro Basketball: Boston defeats Milwaukee in the NBA finals.

College Basketball: North Caroline State defeats Marquette in the NCAA final.

Hockey- Philadelphia Flyers over Boston, Stanley Cup finals.

U.S. Open Tennis-
   Men's Finals: Jimmy Connors beats Ken Rosewall.
   Women's Finals: Billie Jean King beats Evonne Goolagong.

MOVIES- ACADEMY AWARDS

Best Actor: Art Carney, *Harry and Tonto*
Best Actress: Ellen Burstyn, *Alice Doesn't Live Here Anymore*
Best Director: Francis Ford Coppola, *The Godfather, Part II*
Best Picture: *The Godfather, Part II*

CHAPTER XXIX
ONE-HIT WONDERS

Wednesday, October 9, 1974- Memorial Stadium, Baltimore, MD
American League Championship Series, Game Four
Oakland Athletics 2, Baltimore Orioles 1

The Baltimore Orioles were sizzling. They had closed out the 1974 season by winning twenty-nine of their final thirty-five games, including the last nine in a row. When the O's easily beat the Oakland Athletics in the opening game of the American League Championship Series in Oakland, it started to look as if they would run the table all the way to a four-game sweep in the World Series.

Then a funny thing happened on the way to the Series. Baltimore stopped hitting. They were shut out by the Athletics, more affectionately known as the A's, in the second and third games. You can't win if you don't score.

The Birds at least had their home crowd to back them, as they hoped to regroup and capture the lat two games from the two-time defending champion A's. The scene for the fourth, and if necessary, the deciding fifth contest, would be uninspiring Memorial Stadium in Baltimore. The Orioles would try to regain their hitting prowess on their home field, only a stone's throw or a wild pitch from Johns Hopkins University.

Both sides had outstanding starting pitching, and today's starters, Catfish Hunter for Oakland and Mike Cuellar for Baltimore, were two of the finest. Baseball followers anticipated a low-scoring pitcher's duel.

While the Orioles were looking to find their bats, Cuellar seemed to have forgotten where to find home plate. The southpaw normally had good control, but he walked the bases loaded in the first inning, and then managed to work out of the jam.

The game remained scoreless through the first four frames, but Cuellar was leading a charmed life. He walked seven, though he hadn't surrendered a hit. The Oakland batters couldn't reach too many of his deliveries to be able to make contact.

In the A's fifth, Cuellar finally pitched himself out of the game while still not having allowed a hit. He walked four more batters to give Oakland its first run. Cuellar had issued nine free passes in his four and two-thirds innings of hard labor before getting the hook from manager Earl Weaver.

Reliever Ross Grimsley was just as stingy as his predecessor. Oakland was still hitless in Baltimore when they batted in the seventh. The rare possibility of winning a game without the benefit of a base hit now existed in this bizarre contest.

Grimsley issued the eleventh base-on-balls to Sal Bando with one out. The Athletics had received so many walks in the game, they must have thought they had joined a hiking club.

Feared slugger Reggie Jackson then broke up the no-hitter with a double off the left-field fence. The smash just missed clearing the wall, but it did drive in Oakland's second run.

Baltimore came to bat in the ninth trailing by that 2-0 margin. They had not scored a run in thirty innings, stretching back to the eighth inning of the opener. This was their last chance to prolong their season.

The A's completed nine innings of play with only the one hit by Jackson, but the Orioles were not exactly overpowering the baseball. Hunter was working on a neat three-hit shutout, when manager Alvin Dark gave his star right-hander the rest of the afternoon off. He brought in Rollie Fingers, one of a developing new breed of specialists called "Closers." Starters no longer had to pitch complete games as long as a fresh closer could enter the game and blow away the opposition for an inning or two.

Although he was one of a new breed, Fingers looked like an old-timer with his thick handlebar mustache. His appearance on the pitching mound was usually as symbolic as the Boston Celtic basketball coach Red Auerbach lighting up his victory cigar when he was confident his team had won the game.

This time the victory was not so automatic. The Birds, who had a special talent for survival, almost pulled it out. With runners on first and second and the Baltimoreans down to their last out, the ominous Boog Powell slashed a hard single to center for the Orioles' first run in almost a week. On the hit, the club's fifth safety, the tying run was at third base, ninety feet from home plate.

Just as quickly as the sluggish crowd had resuscitated themselves, their hopes flickered away. Fingers did what he was paid to do. He struck out another dangerous batter, Don Baylor, and Oakland was on its way to competing for its third straight World Championship.

Baltimore had out hit the A's five to one, but the one-hit wonders had prevailed in one of the most unusual games the country has ever seen. Tony Bennett may have left his heart in San Francisco, but the Baltimore Orioles must have left their bats in Oakland.

ATHLETICS-ORIOLS RECAP

	R	H	E
Oakland	2	1	0
Baltimore	1	5	1

Winning pitcher- Hunter
Losing pitcher- Cuellar
Save- Fingers
Home runs- none

HERO * Jackson
GOAT < Cuellar

1975

MAJOR HEADLINES

The Suez Canal is reopened after being closed for eight years at the time of the Arab-Israeli War in 1967.

A thirty-five-year-old Japanese woman, Junko Tabei, becomes the first female to climb to the top of Mount Everest.

Two unsuccessful attempts are made on the life of President Ford.

The last remaining Americans are evacuated from Saigon, as Communist forces take over South Vietnam.

Patty Hearst, the publishing heiress who had been kidnapped by the SLA, is captured by the FBI and charged with bank robbery.

SPORTS

Baseball- Cincinnati outlasts Boston in thrilling seven-game World Series.

Pro Football- Pittsburgh Steelers defeat Minnesota in Super Bowl IX. ('74 Season)

College Football: Oklahoma is voted National Champion.

Pro Basketball- Golden State Warriors upset the Washington Bullets for the NBA title.

College Basketball- UCLA defeats Kentucky in the NCAA title game.

Hockey- Philadelphia defeats Buffalo Sabers in the Stanley Cup finals.

U.S. Open Tennis-
    Men's Finals- Manuel Orantes upsets Jimmy Connors.
    Women's Finals: Chris Evert beats Evonne Goolagong.

MOVIES- ACADEMY AWARDS

Best Actor: Jack Nicholson, *One Flew Over the Cuckoo's Nest*
Best Actress: Louise Fletcher, *One Flew Over the Cuckoo's Nest*
Best Director: Milos Forman, *One Flew Over the Cuckoo's Nest*
Best Picture: *One Flew Over the Cuckoo's Nest*

CHAPTER XXX
STAY FAIR, STAY FAIR

Tuesday, October 21, 1975- Fenway Park, Boston, MA
World Series Game Six, Boston Red Sox 7, Cincinnati Reds 6 (12 innings)

When people who love baseball try to recall a really great World Series, they'll usually refer to the 1975 games. The '75 Series between the NL champion Cincinnati Reds and the AL champion Boston Red Sox was one of the great autumn classics of all time. And of all seven games, the most dramatic and exciting was the sixth game, possibly the greatest baseball game ever played.

The Red Sox, led by their brilliant super star, Carl Yastrzemski, and their young center-fielder, Freddie Lynn, who would become both Rookie of the Year and league MVP, were a formidable crew. However, the Ohioans, with Pete Rose, Johnnie Bench, Tony Perez, and Joe Morgan, were near-perfection; they were the Big Red Machine. The Cincinnati Reds in 1975 fielded one of the greatest National League teams in history. Odds makers made them overwhelming favorites to capture their first World Series title since 1940.

When the two clubs left Cincinnati after Game Five, the Reds held a slim lead of three games to two, but looked to complete their business in Boston's venerable Fenway Park.

A spell of terrible weather stopped not only Cincinnati, but Boston as well. Heavy rains struck the New England coast, causing a lengthy postponement of Game Six. During the interminable delay, Fenway Park looked more suitable for canoes than baseballs.

The rain finally stopped, and this provocative World Series resumed after a delay of three days.

The extra days off enabled Red Sox manager Darrell Johnson to start his top right-hander, Luis Tiant for the third time. Tiant had been responsible for both of the Sox' wins and was attempting to become only the thirteenth pitcher to ever win three games in a World Series.

Reds' manager Sparky Anderson countered with another righty, Gary Nolan. Before the night ended, both starters would be long gone, and the contest would see a parade of twelve pitchers marching to and from the mound.

The Bosox electrified the crowd with a huge three-spot in their first turn at bat. After two were out, Yaz and all-star catcher Carlton Fisk each singled, then Fred Lynn, the rookie who played like a ten-year veteran, walloped a long home run into Ted Williams country, the right-center-field bleachers.

Boston could only hold their lead into the fifth stanza. Cincinnati outfielder Ken Griffey smacked a two-run triple off the base of the concrete wall in center. On the play, Lynn twisted his foot while chasing the ball to the wall. The huge crowd fell silent while medics attended to their hero. After about five minutes, he was able to resume his position in center field, and both the crowd and the team heaved a huge sigh of relief.

The Red Machine then tied the game, as Johnny Bench whacked one off the Green Monster in left field. Yastrzemski, who was used to the wall, expertly played the rebound like a racquet ball player and held Bench to a single.

Cincinnati took the lead for the first time in the seventh. Table setters Ken Griffey and Joe Morgan both stroked singles, and after two went down, another heavy-hitting batter, George Foster, crashed a 400-foot double off the wall in deep center field to drive in the runners. When Cesar Geranimo homered in the eighth, the downcast Boston crowd muttered, "Same old Red Sox."

The match was taking on the appearance of a heavyweight title fight as the Bosox took their eighth batting turn. Boston put two men on as pinch-batter Bernie Carbo came to bat. With only four outs to go, the Cincinnati players could already taste the champagne.

Carbo, though, had other ideas. After fouling off several pitches, he found one to his liking and whacked a tremendous home run into the center-field seats to once again deadlock the game. Carbo, who had hit another pinch homer earlier in the Series, tied a record previously set by Chuck Essegian of the Dodgers in 1959. The pair were the only two batters ever to hit two pinch-hit home runs in one World Series.

The Red Sox continued their assault on Cincinnati pitching in the ninth, as they loaded the bases with no one out. The likelihood of a seventh-game showdown appeared inevitable with Fred Lynn striding to the plate.

Lynn lifted a fly ball down the left-field line. Foster crossed the line just into foul territory and made the catch. He then spotted Dennie Doyle, the runner on third, attempting to tag up and score. His throw home was perfect. Bench expertly blocked the plate and tagged a surprised Doyle for a double play. Foster could have let the ball drop, But he was afraid that the wind might blow the ball back into fair territory. When the next hitter, Petrocelli, grounded out, the Reds had dodged a bullet, and this great theatre would continue into extra innings.

Cincy put a runner on first, Ken Griffey, with one down in the top of the eleventh. Their opponents had no hitters to pitch around on this cogent offense, so Joe Morgan waited confidently at the plate. He then smashed a vicious line drive to deep right. This was not Yankee Stadium, where the short porch would yield a sure homer. Everyone in the ballpark was therefore thinking double or triple, which would give the Reds the run that might end the World Series.

The outstanding right-fielder, Dwight Evans, though, did not agree with the assessment. He raced back, and with a turning, twisting leap, made a circus catch in front of the seats for one of the greatest World Series catches in history.

Evans then fired back to first to double up an astounded Griffey and end the inning. Griffey had been running all the way and could not have made it safely back to first if he was driving.

The award-winning movie, *Rocky*, was filming in 1975. As the game moved into the bottom of the twelfth, both squads resembled Rocky Balboa and Apollo Creed as they staggered into the fifteenth round.

Carlton Fisk led off the inning. Johnnie Bench was not the only all-star catcher on the field, and the brilliant Red Sox receiver had made two sparkling defensive plays to display his talents behind the plate. In one, he made a sprawling catch of a Johnnie Bench foul pop, and in the other, he adroitly retrieved a bunt and fired to second to throw out a charging Pete Rose on a sacrifice attempt.

Now it didn't take very long for Fisk to swing into action with his bat. He struck at the second pitch from Pat Darcy, the eighth Cincinnati pitcher, and lofted a fly ball down the foul line, headed toward the netting in left field. The only question was whether it would be fair or foul.

In an image that will forever remain frozen in time, Fisk stood by the baseline waving his arms to the right. "Stay fair, stay fair," he seemed to be pleading.

Carlton received his wish, as the ball struck the foul pole. The Red Sox had won a 7-6 victory in a twelve-inning thriller that both teams later agreed was one of the finest games two teams ever played.

The Fisk homerun made a winner of Rick Wise, the fourth Boston pitcher, who hurled a scoreless twelfth inning. The immortal clout ended a four-hour marathon that lasted until almost one AM.

Both clubs were emotionally drained. The "Refuse to Lose" Red Sox had survived to play another day. The Reds, while disappointed that their quest for the championship had barely eluded them, were nevertheless proud to have been participants in this memorable struggle.

The fans, both at the park and watching on TV, were just as drained as the players and coaches. There would be a lot of tired people going to work later that morning, but those who stayed up until the conclusion (and almost everyone did) were rewarded with some of the most exciting baseball they would ever witness.

The Boston Red Sox haven't won many pennants- this was their ninth; but when they made it to the October Classic, they always provided a terrific show. They were often brilliant in the sixth game of a World Series. Now if they could only learn how to win a seventh.

RED SOX-REDS RECAP

	R	H	E
Boston	7	10	1
Cincinnati	6	14	0

Winning pitcher- Wise
Losing pitcher- Darcy
Home runs- Lynn, Geronimo, Carbo, Fisk

HEROES *** Carbo, Evans, Fisk
GOAT < Darcy

1976

MAJOR HEADLINES

The United States celebrates the 200th birthday of its independence on July 4. The Bicentennial observances include parades, festivals, and a display of tall ships from all over the world in New York Harbor.

Twenty-nine persons are killed by a mysterious "Legionnaire's Disease" while at an American Legion convention at a Philadelphia hotel.

Viking I and II rockets land on Mars to photograph the landscape of the Red Planet.

Former Georgia governor Jimmy Carter narrowly defeats President Ford to capture the White House in the presidential election.

Israeli commandos stage a daring raid to free 105 hostages being held by pro-Palestinian hijackers at the Entebbe Airport in Uganda.

SPORTS

Baseball- Cincinnati sweeps the NY Yankees in the World Series.

Pro Football- Pittsburgh defeats Dallas in Super Bowl X. ('75 Season)

College Football- The National Champion is Pittsburgh University.

Pro Basketball- Boston defeats the Phoenix Suns for the NBA title.

College Basketball- Indiana Beats Michigan for the NCAA championship.

Hockey- Montreal defeats the Philadelphia Flyers in the Stanley Cup finals.

U.S. Open Tennis-
    Men's Finals: Jimmy Connors beats Bjorn Borg.
    Women's Finals: Chris Evert again defeats Evonne Goolagong.

MOVIES- ACADEMY AWARDS

Best Actor: Peter Finch, *Network*
Best Actress: Fay Dunaway, *Network*
Best Director: John G. Avildsen, *Rocky*
Best Picture: *Rocky*

CHAPTER XXXI
CHAMBLIS' GREAT ADVENTURE

Thursday, October 13, 1976- Yankee Stadium, Bronx, NY
American League Championship Series Game Five
New York Yankees 7, Kansas City Royals 6

It was like a long-lost relative returning to visit. The former perennial champion New York Yankees were making their first postseason appearance in twelve years. Some wise trades had filled holes in center field with Mickey Rivers and at second base with Willie Randolph, and strengthened the pitching staff with right-hander Ed Figueroa. Put this together with established stars like Thurman Munson, Graig Nettles, Chris Chamblis, and Catfish Hunter, and the Bombers cruised to an easy Eastern Division title.

Their opponents from the West were a sound but inexperienced Kansas City Royals club. The Royals had been another expansion team that clicked rather quickly. In only their eighth year, they found themselves with a chance to play in the World Series.

The Yankees, with their former sparkplug, Billy Martin, in his first full year as manager, were solid favorites to capture the five-game playoff, but the persistent Royals challenged the New Yorkers through four tough matches. The site for the deciding fifth battle between these two tough rivals would be the newly renovated Yankee Stadium.

The Yankees were happy to be back in their home park after a two-year absence. While the Stadium underwent a major modernization, the Yanks shared Shea Stadium with their cross-town rivals, the Mets.

When it reopened in 1976, the reconstructed Bronx ball yard was a trendy new sports facility. Narrow and sometimes obstructed-view seats were a thing of the past. New, colorful seating and cantilever construction, which eliminated view-blocking posts, made a trip to the ball park a pleasure instead of an annoyance. New escalators whisked patrons quickly and conveniently to their seats. A special section beyond the left-field wall known as Monument Park displayed plaques and monuments as a tribute to the many Yankee legends from the past. The public could visit this well-kept area, which was like an outdoor museum, before the start of each game.

Kansas City had never led this Series in games, but the pair of runs they put up in the opening frame had Yankee players and fans both squirming. Their lead was 3 to 2 after two innings, but the home team took back the lead in the third. Everyone watching just knew that the decision for this game would not come before the ninth inning.

In the sixty stanza, catcher Munson, the league's MVP, singled home a run, and when Chamblis crossed the plate on a throwing error, the New York margin appeared to be a comfortable 6-3.

The Royals had twice trailed the Yanks in games, and as they had done before, they now fought back with stubborn tenacity. In the visitors' eighth, two singles brought the tying run to the plate.

George Brett, the Kansas City third-baseman, was one of baseball's premier hitters, and he didn't disappoint his team at this critical juncture. Brett whacked a long home run to right off reliever Grant Jackson. Jackson had just entered the game to rescue the tiring starter, Ed Figueroa. Brett's homer tied the game and quieted the raucous crowd.

As the contest entered the bottom of the ninth with the score tied at six, the game had to be halted while the grounds crew removed bottles, cans, batteries, and sundry other projectiles that bleacher miscreants were hurling onto the field. The trend towards rowdy behavior at sporting events, especially in New York, had surfaced a few years ago, and visiting players often felt like they were playing in front of the Missing Link.

When play resumed after about ten minutes, first-sacker Chris Chamblis stepped into the batter's box to face the Royals' fifth pitcher, Mark Littell. Chamblis was a contact hitter, who couldn't pass up a pitch he liked.

He must have liked the first pitch, because he creamed it. As he saw the ball disappear over the right-field barrier, Chamblis raised his fist in triumph.

Although the Yankees had won their first pennant since 1964, Chris Chamblis' great adventure had just begun. Hordes of fans swarmed onto the field from all directions. A throng of hoodlums blocked Chamblis' path, and he had to reach out to touch second base, which a fan was already pilfering.

The next obstacle was third base. By now the uncontrollable crowd mobbed the field. Chris made it to third only after the mob knocked him down. He picked himself up and forced his way to the bag like a power fullback. The experience was like trying to cross Central Park at night without being mugged.

The final leg of this perilous journey was the most difficult. Home plate was completely covered by a sea of humanity. He took a circuitous route around the baseline and raced into the dugout, heading toward the safety of the clubhouse.

Chamblis confessed to his jubilant teammates that he wasn't sure if he had touched the plate, since it wasn't visible at the time. Third-baseman Graig Nettles, who had touched home plate thirty-two times after hitting home runs, a figure that led the American League during the season, urged Chamblis to go back out and touch home to ensure that Kansas City could not protest the victory. This he bravely did, but the Royals were only concerned with getting safely to the airport and away from New York as quickly as possible.

The Stadium security finally restored order, and New York fans remembered other heroic clouts by local heroes such as Johnny Lindell, Bobby Thomson, and Dusty Rhodes, that won or led to championships.

Chris Chamblis had surely been a Royal pain, as his eleven hits and eight runs batted in both set records for a league championship playoff. He led all batters with a .524 average and walloped two home runs. The second homer, the pennant-winner, was one of the most spectacular that a member of this storied franchise ever blasted. In the end, the fans did more to try to prevent Chamblis from scoring than the Royals.

YANKEES-ROYALS RECAP

	R	H	E
NY Yankees	7	11	1
Kansas City	6	11	1

Winning pitcher- Tidrow
Losing pitcher- Littell
Home runs- Mayberry, Brett, Chamblis

HERO * Chamblis
GOAT < Littell

1977

MAJOR HEADLINES

President Carter issues a pardon to most of the 10,000 draft evaders, who fled the country during the War in Vietnam.

Convicted murderer Gary Gilmore is executed by a firing squad in Utah. Gilmore becomes the first capital offender to be executed in the United States in ten years.

President Carter signs a bill creating a new cabinet-level Department of Energy.

A massive power blackout similar to the one occurring in 1965 cripples New York City for two days.

The miniseries, Roots, is watched by eighty million viewers, largest viewing audience ever to see a TV program.

SPORTS

Baseball- Yankees defeat the LA Dodgers in six games in the World Series.

Pro Football- Oakland Raiders defeat Minnesota in Super Bowl XI. ('76 Season)

College Football- Notre Dame is the National Champion.

Pro Basketball- Portland Trail Blazers beat the Philadelphia 76ers for the NBA title.

College Basketball- Marquette defeats North Carolina in the NCAA final.

Hockey- Montreal defeats Boston in the Stanley Cup finals.

U.S. Open Tennis-
    Men's Finals: Guillermo Vilas defeats Jimmy Connors.
    Women's Finals: Chris Evert beats Wendy Turnbull for her third straight title.

MOVIES- ACADEMY AWARDS

Best Actor: Richard Dreyfuss, *The Goodbye Girl*
Best Actress: Diane Keaton, *Annie Hall*
Best Director: Woody Allen, *Annie Hall*
Best Picture: *Annie Hall*

CHAPTER XXXII
REGGIE OCTOBER

Tuesday, October 18, 1977- Yankee Stadium, Bronx, NY
World Series Game Six, New York Yankees 8, Los Angeles Dodgers 4

The Yankees and Dodgers were renewing acquaintances in 1977 in another transcontinental World Series. The last time the two combatants met was in 1963, when the Californians swept the New Yorkers in four games.

Yankee manager Billy Martin won his second pennant in his second full season leading the team. Freshman manager Tom Lasorda, who succeeded long-time skipper Walter Alston, won the flag in his first try with the Dodgers.

After falling behind in games 3 to 1 in Los Angeles, Lasorda had to be encouraged with the 10-4 trouncing his squad inflicted on the Yanks in the fifth game. As his warriors prepared to do battle in Game Six at Yankee Stadium on a cool October evening, Lasorda was hoping his club would gain the momentum to sweep the remaining games in the Bronx. The Dodgers no longer played in Brooklyn, and the World Series jinx that had so long prevailed appeared to have dissolved with their move to the West Coast.

The hot-hitting Dodgers picked up where they left off in the previous game, as they opened with two runs in their first batting turn. Their dependable first-baseman, Steve Garvey tripled in the runs.

The wind was blowing out to right, and the left-handed hitters took advantage of the short porch in right field by playing Home Run Derby. Chris Chamblis for the Yankees and Reggie Smith for the Dodgers connected, and as the game entered the bottom of the fourth, Los Angeles held a one-run lead.

The turning point of the game came in that frame. After Thurman Munson led off with a single, the flamboyant right-fielder, Reggie Jackson, came to bat. He drilled the first pitch off started Burt Hooton into the seats in right. The Bronx Bombers led for the first time, a lead they would not relinquish.

The Yanks doubled their advantage moments later on a manufactured run. The pesky Chamblis doubled, advanced to third on an infield grounder, and scored on an outfield fly ball.

The next inning, Mickey Rivers singled, and up came Reggie. This time Elia Sosa was the pitcher, but the result was the same. Jackson crushed the first pitch for a home run, and the New York lead had escalated to 7-3.

Jackson came to bat once again in the eighth with his team still holding a four-run bulge. His mound opponent was now knuckle-ball specialist Charley Hough. The knuckler is a hard pitch to hit squarely, because it flutters like a butterfly. Jackson, though, timed it just right.

He didn't want to hurt Hough's feelings, so he again hit the first pitch. This time the ball went even further than the other two. It sailed into the dark, unused area of the center field bleachers, where the seats remain unsold to provide a better background for hitters. The ball traveled about 450 feet. Three pitches, three homers, and the Yankees were three outs from capturing their first World Championship in fifteen years.

The ninth inning was déjà vu. Fans began to throw all kinds of foreign objects onto the field, including dangerous firecrackers. Jackson had to leave his post in right field to secure a batting helmet, which he then wore to protect himself. The scene bore a resemblance to the final ALCS game against Kansas City the previous October.

Yankee hurler Mike Torrez was on the verge of winning his second route-going victory in this World Series battle. Although he yielded a run in the ninth inning, the Dodgers' fourth, and had given up nine hits, manager Martin wanted to get the game over with and get his team safely off the field.

With two out, Torrez faced pinch-hitter Lee Lacy. Frenzied fans perched on the top of the right field wall. The scene was like a remake of Alfred Hitchcock's scary movie, *The Birds*, only the antagonists this time were human. The players may have wished to reassess that evaluation, however.

As Lacy popped up an attempted bunt that Torrez snared near the mound, the crowd surged onto the field. Last year it was Chamblis, and this time it was Jackson's turn to run for his life. Reggie ran like Franco Harris, stiff-arming fans on both sides. After leading the Yankees in batting, he now led the club in rushing yardage.

Both teams made it to their respective clubhouses without further incident. The New York Yankees had won their first World Series since their memorable 1-0, seventh-game win over the Giants in 1962.

Reggie Jackson loved the spotlight and seemed to thrive when he had the nation's attention thrust upon him. George Steinbrenner, the controversial owner of the new World Champions, was so impressed with Reggie Jackson's performance that he named him "Mr. October."

Indeed Reggie October had provided one of the greatest offensive displays that a Fall Classic ever produced. It didn't matter whether the pitcher's name was Hooton, Sosa, or Hough. His three circuits on three pitches were like three rifle shots.

Reggie had become the only man to perform the hat trick other than Babe Ruth, who homered three times in a World Series game in 1926 and again in 1928. Jackson was also the first player to ever hit five home runs in a World Series.

The New Yorkers had finally extracted revenge for the '63 whitewashing they suffered at the hands of their former tormentors. The 1963 Yankees didn't have Reggie Jackson, but the 1977 Dodgers didn't have Sandy Koufax either.

YANKEES-DODGERS RECAP

	R	H	E
Yanks	8	8	1
Los Angeles	4	9	0

Winning pitcher- Torrez
Losing pitcher- Hooton
Home runs- Chamblis, Smith, Jackson 3

HERO * Jackson
GOAT < Hough

1978

MAJOR HEADLINES

U.S. Senate votes to have Panama take over control of the Panama Canal.

Voters in California overwhelmingly approve "Proposition 13," which slashes property taxes in that state.

Israeli Prime Minister Begin and Egyptian President Sadat meet with President Carter at Camp David to sign an unprecedented peace agreement between the two nations.

Pope John Paul II from Poland is the first non-Italian in 455 years to be elevated to the Papacy in a ceremony in St. Peters Square in the Vatican.

SPORTS

Baseball: Yankees again defeat the Dodgers in the World Series in six games.

Pro Football: Dallas beats the Denver Broncos in Super Bowl XII. ('77 Season)

College Football: Alabama and Southern California share the National Title.

Pro Basketball: Washington wins the NBA title from the Seattle Sonics.

College Basketball: Kentucky defeats Duke for the NCAA championship.

Hockey: Montreal again defeats Boston for third straight Stanley Cup title.

U.S. Open Tennis-
    Men's Finals: Jimmy Connors beats Bjorn Borg.
    Women's Finals: Chris Evert takes fourth straight title defeating Pam Shriver.

MOVIES- ACADEMY AWARDS

Best Actor: Jon Voight, *Coming Home*

Best Actress: Jane Fonda, *Coming Home*

Best Director: Michael Dimino, *The Deer Hunter*

Best Picture: *The Deer Hunter*

CHAPTER XXXIII
BUCKY DENTS THE SCREEN

Monday, October 1, 1978- Fenway Park, Boston, MA
American League Eastern Division Playoff Game
New York Yankees 5, Boston Red Sox 4

The cities of New York and Boston have developed a rivalry in professional sports over the years that is second to none. In basketball, the Knicks and Celtics have had many classic battles fighting for supremacy in the NBA.

Now the Yankees and Red Sox have revived a tempestuous rivalry that developed back in the Forties, as both teams had again become the dominant American League powers in 1978. Boston led the New Yorkers by fourteen games in late July, but the Bombers caught and passed the Sox in mid-September. The clubs battled down to the final game of the season in one of baseball's most exciting pennant races. When the Yankees lost that Sunday game while the Red Sox won, the American League would need its second tiebreaker to settle the Eastern Division championship.

The Red Sox were also involved in the other first-place tie, losing to Cleveland in 1948. Boston had won the coin toss for home field, and the one-game playoff at old Fenway Park would become a remarkable performance, with heroics on both sides. The contest would play on a brilliantly sunny Monday afternoon. A decision on the team that would advance to the League Championship games would not come until the final pitch, one of the truly greatest games of all time.

Yankee manager Bob Lemon had his ace left-hander, Ron Guidry, ready for mound chores. Guidry was baseball's dominant pitcher in 1978, leading the majors in strikeouts and earned-run average, while posting an astounding 25-3 record.

Bosox manager Don Zimmer chose a tough right-hander, Mike Torres. Ironically, Torrez had been the Yankee pitching star of the '77 World Series, winning two games. He was hurling the clincher, when Reggie Jackson walloped his three circuit blasts. The call to free agency, though, beckoned, and Torrez signed a lucrative contract with Boston. He immediately became one of the mainstays on their starting staff.

Through the first six innings, Torrez' performance had overshadowed that of his more celebrated opponent. While he had limited the Yankees to just two hits, two of the Boston heroes, Carl Yastrzemski and Jim Rice, drove in runs that gave the Red Sox a 2-0 lead. Yaz homered in the second inning, and Rice, the most lethal hitter in the league all year, drove in Rick Burleson, who had doubled, in the sixth.

In the visitors' seventh, the New Yorkers realized they only had three innings to keep alive their season. Chris Chamblis and Roy White both singled, but with two out, the light-hitting shortstop, Bucky Dent, came to the plate. Lemon was thin in infield reserves with second-baseman Willie Randolph out with a leg injury, so he allowed Dent to bat.

Bucky had hit only four home runs all season, but the demons that were punishing the Boston Red Sox since they sold Babe Ruth to the Yankees in 1919 were apparently unforgiving. The Bosox had not won a World Championship since 1918, and their fans feared that there was still time for them to find a way to lose this one.

Dent hoisted a fly ball that struck the screen above the left-field wall. His fifth home run was about as popular in New England as the Boston Massacre.

Zimmer lifted Torrez after one more batter, as Mickey Rivers drew a walk. He called on Bob Stanley, who had a 15-2 record while doubling as a starter and reliever. Thurman Munson welcomed Stanley into the game quite rudely. The Yankee catcher doubled in the fourth run of the inning.

The Yanks didn't expect the long-ball support they obtained from Bucky Dent, but they weren't surprised when Reggie Jackson walloped a long home run. His eighth-inning blast upped the New York advantage to three runs.

When Guidry tired in the seventh inning, Goose Gossage took the call from the pen to try to preserve the win as he had done all year. The Goose was not as overpowering as usual, and he struggled through a gutsy eighth-inning.

Both Yaz and Fred Lynn had RBI singles to shave the lead to one precious run, but Gossage pitched out of a potentially damaging jam. With two on and one out, he retired Butch Hobson on a fly ball to right and struck out George Scott.

The game, the season, and eventual World Championship came down to the last of the ninth. Boston only trailed 5-4, as Burleson walked with one down.

One of the most controversial moves that Lemon had made since succeeding Billy Martin as the New York manager during the summer was to replace superstar Reggie Jackson in right field with the steadier defensive player, Lou Piniella. Jackson took Piniella's place as the designated hitter, and continued to bat cleanup. The move was about to pay dividends, as the veteran would make two clutch defensive plays to save at least the tying, and possibly winning runs from scoring.

The next batter, Jerry Remy, lined to right. Right field at Fenway Park is one of the worst sun fields in the majors, similar to left field at Yankee Stadium. On this day, with a cloudless blue sky, Piniella could not locate the ball. Lou moved back several steps, hoping to keep the ball in front of him, and pounded his glove as if he was getting ready to make the catch.

The decoy worked, as Burleson didn't start to run right away, waiting to see if it would be caught. The ball landed a few feet away from Piniella, and Burleson could only reach second base. Lou picked up the ball and fired a perfect throw to third, just in case the Boston shortstop had any ideas of taking the extra base.

Lou Piniella's battles with the sun continued. Jim Rice, the man who would become the American League MVP, then lifted another fly to deep right. At first the struggling outfielder couldn't see the ball again. He didn't want to lose the pennant on Rice's forty-seventh home run, and fortunately for him, he finally spotted the descending sphere and caught it in front of the wall.

Burleson tagged up and went to third. If not for Piniella's cleverly deceptive play on the previous batter, the game would now be tied.

Thus it all came down to a classic confrontation-Yastrzemski versus Gossage. Runners were on first and third, two were out. The mighty Yaz, whose homer and single had driven in half of the Bosox runs, was in his late thirties, but, like a great wine, seemed to be getting better with age.

This time, however, the ageless star couldn't make it happen again. Yaz tried to check his swing on a ball delivered in on his fists but couldn't. Gossage threw him a fast ball that tailed in, and he popped it up into four territory behind third base. It seemed like an eternity, but a few seconds later, Nettles squeezed the ball in his glove, and the Yankees had survived to win a sensational 5-4 victory. Goose had not pitched one of his better games in relief, but he toiled well enough to get the job done.

The Yankees and Red Sox were by far the two best teams in the major leagues in 1978. It seemed unfair that one of these super squads would have to go home after losing one winner-take-all battle by one run, with the potential tying and winning runs on base.

It was also likely that, had the Red Sox won this classic, they would have gone on to easily defeat Kansas City in the ALCS and the Dodgers in the World Series just as the Yankees had done.

After the game, Reggie Jackson stated in the victors' locker room that it was a shame that they couldn't take along the Bosox to the League Championship and the World Series. That would be quite a frightening thought, as a roster that combined players from both these clubs might never lose another game.

YANKEES-RED SOX RECAP

	R	H	E
New York	5	8	0
Boston	4	11	0

Winning pitcher- Guidry
Losing pitcher- Torrez
Home runs- Yastrzemski, Dent, Jackson

HEROES *** Dent, Piniella, Gossage
GOAT < Burleson

1979

MAJOR HEADLINES

Iranian militants seize the U.S. Embassy in Tehran and take ninety people hostage, including sixty-three Americans.

A nuclear reactor in Three Mile Island in Pennsylvania has a partial meltdown, releasing radioactive material into the air.

The federal government announces a $1.5 billion loan plan to help bail out the financially-troubled Chrysler Corporation.

Americans looking to buy gasoline again see more shortages and long lines at the pump.

SPORTS

Baseball: Pittsburgh edges Baltimore in a seven-game World Series.

Pro Football: Pittsburgh Steelers beat Dallas in Super Bowl XIII. ('78 Season)

College Football: Alabama wins the National Championship.

Pro Basketball: Seattle defeats Washington in the NBA finals.

College Basketball: Michigan State defeats Indiana State in the NCAA finals.

Hockey: Montreal defeats the New York Rangers in the Stanley Cup finals.

U.S. Open Tennis-
    Men's Finals: John McEnroe defeats Vitas Gerulaitis
    Women's Finals: Tracy Austin defeats Chris Evert Lloyd.

MOVIES- ACADEMY AWARDS

Best Actor: Dustin Hoffman, *Kramer vs. Kramer*
Best Actress: Sally Fields, *Norma Rae*
Best Director: Robert Benton, *Kramer vs. Kramer*
Best Picture: *Kramer vs. Kramer*

CHAPTER XXXIV
ONE FOR THE FAMILY

Wednesday, October 17, 1979- Memorial Stadium, Baltimore, MD
World Series Game Seven, Pittsburgh Pirates 4, Baltimore Orioles 1

Two of baseball's traditionally strong squads, the Pittsburgh Pirates and the Baltimore Orioles, were staging a reunion in the 1979 World Series. The Pirates won the last meeting between the two in seven games in 1971.

The Orioles had raced to a commanding three-to-one lead in games, but Pittsburgh came storming back to take the next two. Fans love when a World Series goes seven, and tonight at Baltimore's Memorial Stadium, they would be getting their wish.

Among the capacity crowd in attendance was the president of the United States, Jimmy Carter. Carter was the first president to attend a World Series contest since Dwight Eisenhower witnessed a game at Ebbets Field in Brooklyn in 1956. The president was taking an evening off from dealing with the double-digit inflation that now plagued the nation.

The Pirates of 1979 were a close-knit bunch, who referred to themselves as "The Family." If they were a family, then their patriarch was the man they called "Pops," Willie Stargell. The thirty-eight year old slugging first-baseman was an inspiration to his teammates both on and off the field. Stargell's leadership had played a major roll in Pittsburgh's march to the NL pennant, and he had become a significant force in these October games.

Nobody could blame President Carter for cheering when second-baseman Rich Dauer homered for the Birds in the third inning off Pirate starter Jim Bibby. Baltimore was the closest thing to a home team for the people who lived or worked in the Nation's Capital.

The run was holding up, as lefty Scott McGregor kept the hard-hitting Bucs from crossing the plate through five strong innings. It was Willie Stargell, though, who was about to change the complexion of this game and Series.

With a runner, outfielder Bill Robinson, on first by way of a single, Stargell smashed the first pitch over the fence in right. The blast quieted the crowd, as they realized the visitors now led for the first time.

The Pirate bullpen had depth, and the Orioles knew that they would run out of time if they couldn't revive their slumbering bats. In the eighth, Baltimore loaded the bases with two out, but the dangerous Eddie Murray stranded the runners with a long fly out to the right-field fence.

With an inning to go, Pittsburgh worked on adding to its lead to give them some breathing room. Omar Moreno, the swift center-fielder, drove in a run with his third hit of the night. Another run crossed the plate when Pitcher Dennis Martinez hit Robinson with the bases loaded. The 4-1 cushion appeared to be enough to bring the fifth World Series crown to the Pittsburgh franchise.

In a classic case of over management, Oriole manager Earl Weaver paraded five pitchers to the mound to try to stop the Pirates from inflicting any further damage. The quintet of Tim Stoddard, Mike Flanagan, Don Stanhouse, Tippy Martinez, and Dennis Martinez, who all worked the top of the ninth, set a World Series record for the most pitchers a team used in an inning. During this interminable stanza, Weaver made so many trips to the mound, he must have thought there was a salad bar out there.

The end for Baltimore came shortly thereafter. Pat Kelly lofted a fly ball to center, which Moreno squeezed for the final out of the ninth inning and the final play of the Series. Pittsburgh was the City of Champions, as the Steelers had won the Super Bowl earlier in the year, and now the Pirates were champs of the baseball world. Manager Chuck Tanner would happily accept the World Series trophy and personal congratulations from President Carter in the locker room.

No one could guess the outcome of the decisive game until Willie Stargell popped one for the Family. When their leader took charge, the rest of the team responded in a manner that would insure victory.

Pops was easily the outstanding player of the '79 Series. He had four hits in the crucial seventh game, including the gamer. He finished with a lofty .400 batting average in the seven games, including three homeruns. His seven extra-base hits were a World Series record.

The Pirates became only the fourth team to overcome a three-games-to-one handicap and bounce back to win. Another Pittsburgh club, the 1925 edition, also accomplished this minor miracle. The Bucs had some elite company, the 1958 New York Yankees and the 1968 Detroit Tigers, who also had to win the last three.

In the end, the Pirates were able to rally and win partly because their offense cranked it up and finished strong, while the Oriole bats disappeared after the fourth game.

Pittsburgh had a collective .323 batting mark. This awesome display of lumber was the second highest team average in World Series history, eclipsed only by the 1960 Yankees against these same Bucs.

Conversely, Baltimore could only knock out four hits in the final seventh game. In their last three battles, the losers produced two runs and seventeen hits. This exercise in futility was a significant factor in the evaporation of such a once-comfortable advantage.

PIRATES-ORIOLES RECAP

	R	H	E
Pittsburgh	4	11	0
Baltimore	1	4	2

Winning pitcher- Jackson
Losing pitcher- McGregor
Home runs- Dauer, Stargell

HERO * Stargell
GOAT < Weaver (manager)

1980

MAJOR HEADLINES

President Carter announces economic sanctions against the Soviet Union in retaliation for the Soviet takeover of Afghanistan. He also urges the US Olympic Committee to boycott the Summer Olympic Games in Moscow.

Mount Saint Helens, the volcano in Washington State, erupts three times in one week, killing fifty-seven.

Ronald Reagan soundly defeats incumbent President Carter to secure the White House.

John Lennon, the former member of the Beatles, is shot and killed outside his apartment in New York City.

SPORTS

Baseball: Philadelphia Phillies defeat Kansas City Royals in the World Series.

Pro Football: Pittsburgh beats Los Angeles Rams in Super Bowl XIV ('79 season)

College Football: Georgia wins the National Championship.

Pro Basketball: Los Angeles defeats Philadelphia in NBA finals.

College Basketball: Louisville beats UCLA in NCAA finals.

Hockey: New York Islanders defeat Philadelphia in Stanley Cup finals.

U.S. Open Tennis-
    Men's Finals: John McEnroe beats Bjorn Borg.
    Women's Finals: Chris Evert Lloyd beats Hana Mandlikova

MOVIES- ACADEMY AWARDS

Best Actor: Robert DeNiro, *Raging Bull*
Best Actress: Sissy Spacek, *Coal Miner's Daughter*
Best Director: Robert Redford, *Ordinary People*
Best Picture: *Ordinary People*

CHAPTER XXXV
NEW FACES OF 1980

Sunday, October 12, 1980- Astrodome, Houston, TX
National League Championship Series, Game Five
Philadelphia Phillies 8, Houston Astros 7 (10 innings)

The Philadelphia Phillies had won only two pennants in their history. They had not made a World Series appearance since Robin Roberts had pitched and Dick Sisler had batted them into the Fall Classic back in 1950. After having lost three National League Championship Series, the Phils were now attempting to win their first pennant in thirty years.

The Houston Astros had entered the National League with the New York Mets as expansion teams in 1962. Having won the Western Division race, this was the Astros' first entry into postseason play. This LCS was also the first to hold games indoors, as the scene for the last three contests was the Astrodome, named for the Astronaut-training Space Center in Houston.

The winner of this series would meet another expansion club, the Kansas City Royals. The Royals awaited the survivor of this protracted playoff, after having surprised the baseball world by sweeping the New York Yankees in three games in the American League Championship Series.

The Phillies and Astros didn't seem to want their LCS to end. As they prepared for a showdown fifth game at the Astrodome, they had been forced to play extra innings in the last three encounters. The adversaries were about to work overtime for the fourth straight time before the foes provided a winner. Both benches truly displayed an element of fatigue.

When the Astros broke a 2-2 tie in the home seventh, it looked like the prelude to an all-expansion World Series. Marty Bystrom, a rookie right-hander, who had joined the Phils on September 1, was the emergency starter. No one else on the staff was able to raise his arm to volunteer to pitch.

Dennie Walling singled in the lead run off reliever Larry Christenson. When Christenson threw a wild pitch, the second run crossed the plate. Art Howe then found the gap in right-center, and the ball kept rolling on the carpet. The triple gave Houston their third run of the inning and lit up the capacity crowd at the Dome.

With their best hurler, strikeout king Nolan Ryan, the Astros took a 5 to 2 lead into the eighth and looked like a lock. Philadelphia looked like a team about to lose their fourth playoff in five years. The Stros didn't count on both Ryan and the rest of the pen running out of gas.

Philly loaded the bases on three hits to open the inning. The key hit was Larry Bowa's smash off Ryan's glove. If Ryan was able to hold onto the bullet, he would have probably started a double play. When Greg Gross beat out a bunt, Ryan's night was over.

The Phillies continued to attack the relievers. Pete Rose walked to score one run. An infield force out scored a second. The dangerous Mike Schmidt then struck out, but Del Unser's pinch single tied the game.

Outfielder Manny Trillo, who would later win the MVP award of this NLCS, tripled in the fourth and fifth runs of the inning. Philadelphia now had the lead 7 to 5, but this was starting to look like the finish of a wild NFL game, where the last team to get the ball usually wins. Somebody on one of these squads must have been able to kick.

Upset at their failure to hold on to their lead late in the game, Houston struck back when they took their turn at bat. They bunched four straight hits for a pair of runs to once again tie the game.

Phillie reliever Tug McGraw, the former Met hero, was appearing in his fifth straight game but failed to stop the Texans this time. With two on and two out, clutch safeties by Rafael Landestoy and Jose Cruz drove in the runs that evened the count and threw the National League flag up for grabs. A scoreless ninth inning then forced this exhausting final into overtime once again.

Del Unser, who had pinch-hit to drive in a run in the Phillies' big eighth-inning rally, stayed in the game to play center field and again contributed a vital blow in the tenth inning. He led off with a double and scored when Garry Maddox stroked another two-base-hit to give Philadelphia the advantage, the fourth lead change of this see-saw struggle.

The Phils gave the ball to Dick Ruthven, a starter in the rotation, who was making his first relief appearance of the season. Ruthvan was one of the few pitchers whose arm hadn't yet fallen off. He took over in the ninth and retired all six Houston batters he faced to gain the victory that finally gave the Red Quakers their third pennant.

Although their heroes had been beaten, the Astro fans stood up and enthusiastically applauded both teams for their performance during the past week. There were no losers in this playoff. Both clubs earned the respect of the whole nation, who had witnessed a hard-fought battle second to none.

The Phillies were on the verge of elimination after their third-game defeat at the Astrodome. Having to win two in a row in front of a hostile crowd seemed like a monumental task, which worsened with the club trailing by a pair of runs with six outs to go in Game Four.

They rallied to take the lead in the eighth inning, just as they did in the deciding battle. Houston tied it in the ninth, but Philadelphia won it in the tenth inning, just as they had done tonight.

An exhausted Phillie squad would have one day off before facing a well-rested Kansas City club, but after the way they had twice overcome certain defeat to win on the road, it would come as no surprise when they eventually won their first World Championship. The Philadelphia fans were so elated, they probably would have sounded the Liberty Bell again if it wasn't locked up.

PHILLIES-ASTROS RECAP

	R	H	E
Philadelphia	8	13	2
Houston	7	11	0

Winning pitcher- Ruthven
Losing pitcher- LaCorte
Home runs- none

HEROES *** Trillo, Unser, Ruthven
GOATS <<< Houston bullpen

1981

MAJOR HEADLINES

The Americans held hostage in Iran for 444 days are released moments after President Reagan is inaugurated. The new president sends outgoing President Carter to Germany to meet the hostages when they arrive there.

President Reagan, Press Secretary James Brady, a Secret Service agent, and a policeman are shot and seriously wounded outside a Washington, DC hotel. John Hinckley Jr. is arrested but later committed to a mental institution by reason of insanity.

Congress passes President Reagan's massive tax cut bill, which is expected to save taxpayers about $750 billion over the next five years.

Federal air traffic controllers begin an illegal nationwide strike. Most of the workers are dismissed by the president after they defy a back-to work order.

The Royal Wedding of Prince Charles and Lady Diana takes place at St. Paul's Cathedral in London.

The US Senate confirms the appointment of Sandra Day O'Connor as the first women Supreme Court Justice.

SPORTS

Baseball: Dodgers defeat NY Yankees in a six-game World Series.

Pro Football: Oakland beats Philadelphia Eagles in Super Bowl XV. ('80 season)

College Football: Clemson is voted National Champion.

Pro Basketball: Boston defeats Houston Rockets in NBA finals.

College Basketball: Indiana beats North Carolina in NCAA final.

Hockey: NY Islanders win second straight Stanley Cup by beating Minnesota.

U.S. Open Tennis-
    Men's Finals: John McEnroe defeats Bjorn Borg.
    Women's Finals: Tracy Austin defeats Martina Navratilova

MOVIES- ACADEMY AWARDS

Best Actor: Henry Fonda, *On Golden Pond*
Best Actress: Katherine Hepburn, *On Golden Pond*
Best Director: Warren Beatty, *Reds*
Best Picture: *Reds*

CHAPTER XXXVI
BLUE MONDAY IN MONTREAL

Monday, October 19, 1981- Olympic Stadium, Montreal QUE, CAN
National League Championship Series, Game Five
Los Angeles Dodgers 2, Montreal Expos 1

They sat huddled together in warm clothing in forty-degree temperatures. The fans at Montreal's Olympic Stadium looked more like they were awaiting the arrival of Santa Clause than the start of a baseball game.

Yet none of the spectators who filled the stadium, former site of the 1976 Summer Olympics, would trade places with anyone who couldn't get a seat. They were all there to see history made. If their adored Expos could defeat the National League West Champion Los Angeles Dodgers today, the 1981 World Series would make its first-ever appearance in Canada.

The NL Final moved from sunny California to chilly Montreal for the third game, and the Expos triumphed to excite the Canadian fans. Nobody believed the Dodgers could take two straight on the road, no less in another country, and the fans couldn't wait to celebrate.

Los Angeles managed to win the fourth game, but after waiting three and a half hours, drenching rains postponed the fifth-game showdown on a soggy Sunday afternoon. Thus, like the previous NLCS in 1980, another thrilling battle was about to start. This tense struggle wouldn't produce the '81 pennant winner until the final out of the game.

The rain finally stopped, and the grounds crew could cancel their plans to construct an arc. Since the survivor didn't want to be late for a World Series appointment at Yankee Stadium the following night, the Monday matinee finally began with heavy tension on both benches.

The starting pitchers, Fernando Valenzuela for LA and Ray Burris for Montreal, were also the mound foes in game two. In that one, Burris bested Valenzuela, the Dodgers' outstanding rookie. Both hurlers would pitch brilliantly, with Burris tossing eight innings of five-hit ball. Valenzuela, the young Mexican lefty and eventual Rookie of the Year and Cy Young winner, limited the Expos to three safeties in eight and two-thirds innings.

The Expos scored first in the opening frame. Speedster Tim Raines led with a double, went to third on a safe bunt by Rodney Scott, and scored on a double play, which short-circuited a potentially big inning.

The Dodgers tied it in the fifth. Outfielders Rick Monday and Pedro Guerrero opened with singles, putting runners at the corners with nobody out. Burris then bounced a wild pitch into the dirt. Guerrero raced to second, but a smart play by the catcher, Gary Carter, held Monday on third base. Carter deflected the errant delivery towards third base, preventing Monday from coming home.

Valenzuela then helped his own cause by getting the RBI with a ground out. But had Burris not thrown the wild pitch, the grounder would have probably resulted in an inning-ending double play.

As the pitching ruled, both clubs seemed anxious to stay off the field and keep warm in their respective dugouts. There were no more scoring threats through the eighth inning.

In the ninth, Expo manager Jim Fanning surprised everyone by removing Burris and replacing him with another starter, Steve Rogers. Burris had not shown any signs of tiring, but Fanning had seen Rogers pitch four strong wins in a row at the end of the season, allowing just two runs in his last thirty-six innings.

The fact that would later motivate second-guessers was that Rogers had exclusively been a starter for the Expos. He hadn't worked in relief in over three years.

Fanning later tried to justify his questionable move by stating that Rogers was his ace, and you win games with your best. Besides he had his super closer, Jeff Reardon, warming up just in case he needed him.

Rogers got two quick outs, and it looked like Montreal would try to cop the flag in sudden death. The third batter, however, was the thirty-five-year-old veteran, Rick Monday, who scored the lone Dodger run. Rogers, a sinker-ball specialist, tried to throw a sinker now, only it didn't sink quickly enough. When Monday connected, the ball instead sailed over the center-field fence before finally sinking to the ground.

The blow shocked fans all over Canada, as they started to see their thirteen-year dream of a Canadian World Series begin to fade. Nevertheless, the Expos still had a final shot in the bottom of the ninth, so they hadn't lost hope.

As in the top half of the inning, Valenzuela retired the first two batters. He looked to wrap up the win with an impressive complete-game victory. Fernando, however, was showing the stress of the tense struggle on this frosty afternoon, and he lost the next two batters on bases on balls.

Manager Tom Lasorda, w ho had already won two pennants in his first four years in Tinsel Town, didn't want to lose this opportunity to secure number three. He summoned Bob Welch from the bullpen to preserve the win.

Welch had to face right-fielder Jerry White, whose hit had won the third game putting the Expos on the mountain peak they couldn't quite surmount. White softly grounded out to second, ending the dream at least for this year.

The second straight thrilling NLCS had ended, and in each case, it was a shame that one of the teams had to go home. The play in both leagues had been crisp down the stretch. This was fortunate, since a damaging players strike that suspended play for six weeks had victimized the game.

The strike, based on a labor dispute between millionaire ball players and owners, had alienated the fans, and the only way to recapture them would be for the players to show intense effort on the field when they returned. This they did, and the games in Los Angeles and Montreal were an example of how the sport was starting to regain its popularity.

The Montreal Expos had entered the National League in 1969. Their success on the field followed the Mets and Astros as fledgling teams to earn postseason appearances in their brief existence in the National League. Although one pitch had created a blue Monday in Montreal, the club now knew that it could compete with the best of the league and looked forward to taking its success to the next level.

DODGERS-EXPOS RECAP

	R	H	E
Los Angeles	2	6	0
Montreal	1	3	1

Winning pitcher- Valenzuela
Losing pitcher- Rogers
Home run- Monday

HERO * Monday
GOAT < Rogers

1982

MAJOR HEADLINES

After a ten-year battle, the Equal Rights Amendment is finally defeated.

The Unemployment rate in the United States reaches eleven per-cent, highest since 1940.

Barney Clark, a retired dentist, is the recipient of the world's first artificial heart.

A glut in global oil causes gasoline prices to tumble.

SPORTS

Baseball: St. Louis defeats the Milwaukee Brewers in a seven-game World Series.

Pro Football: San Francisco 49ers defeat the Cincinnati Bengals in Super Bowl XVI.
            ('81 Season)

College Football: Penn State is the National Champion.

Pro Basketball: Los Angeles defeats Philadelphia in the NBA finals.

College Basketball: North Carolina beats Georgetown in the NCAA final.

Hockey: NY Islanders beat Vancouver to win their third straight Stanley Cup.

U.S. Open Tennis-
    Men's Finals: Jimmy Connors defeats Ivan Lendle.
    Women's Finals: Chris Evert Lloyd defeats Hana Mandlikova.

MOVIES- ACADEMY AWARDS

Best Actor: Ben Kingsley, *Gandhi*
Best Actress: Meryl Streep, *Sophie's Choice*
Best Director: Richard Attenborough, *Gandhi*
Best Picture: *Gandhi*

CHAPTER XXXVII
A POTENT BREW

Sunday, October 10, 1982- County Stadium, Milwaukee, WI
American League Championship Series, Game Five
Milwaukee Brewers 4, California Angels 3

The recent success of expansion teams in the National League was also occurring with American League neophytes. The Kansas City Royals, formed in 1969, won the 1980 pennant. Now the other club to enter the AL that year, the former Seattle Pilots transformed into the Milwaukee Brewers, was battling the California Angels in the League Playoff.

The Angels had entered the league back in 1962, when the American League followed the National League to the West Coast. Since the two dominant teams in the Junior Circuit in 1982 were clubs that hadn't existed little more than two decades ago, the '82 World Series would definitely have its second expansion representative from the Junior Circuit.

The Angels were a formidable group, led by All-Stars Reggie Jackson, Rod Carew, Fred Lynn, and Don Baylor. They had a solid lineup from one to nine.

The Brewers of 1982, however were an awesome offensive club. Led by Paul Molitor, Cecil Cooper, Gorman Thomas, and eventual MVP Robin Yount, the Milwaukee squad stirred a potent brew that averaged almost six runs per game. Four players drove in over a hundred runs, and a fifth just missed the century mark with ninety-seven.

Milwaukee hoped to become the first team to capture a league championship after losing the first two games since baseball established the format in 1969. California had taken the first two at their sunny home near Disneyland, but the Brew Crew stormed back to win the next two on their Wisconsin field. Thus another fifth-game showdown was about to occur on a chilly Sunday afternoon at County Stadium.

The Angels picked up the early advantage in the exciting contest. After their fourth at-bat, they led 3-1. Becoming jealous of the rival Dodger success, they were starting to believe that, like the Dodgers, the American League would soon bring the World Series to Southern California.

Center-fielder Fred Lynn, the former Red Sox star, twice singled in a run. Lynn, who was now happy to be playing in his home state, would become the ALCS most valuable player by accumulating a record-shattering .611 batting average in the five-game playoff. He would become the first player so honored from the losing team.

Ben Oglivie, the Brewers' slugging left-fielder, retaliated with a powerful home run to keep the game close. The score was 3 to 2 at the seventh-inning stretch.

Although the Brewers lived by the long-ball all season, the autumn chill in Milwaukee prevented balls from carrying well. If Harvey's Wallbangers, the name the press gave them in honor of their manager, Harvey Kuenn, were to pull out this game, they would have to manufacture some runs with care and precision.

The Brewer fans sat down, and right-fielder Charlie Moore topped one into the dirt that Cal second-baseman Bobbie Grich tried to scoop up but could only trap. It was an infield single, but just as effective as if it had been a line drive.

Jim Gantner followed with another single, and, with two out, Robin Yount drew a walk to fill the sacks for Cecil Cooper.

The first-baseman was the consummate professional. His season statistics- .313 batting average, thirty-two homers, and 121 runs batted in, were typical, in that he always hit for average and power and was defensively solid around the bag

Nevertheless, Cooper was having a horrendous Championship Series. He was only two for nineteen and struck out six times. What could be a better time to redeem himself than now with the pennant hanging in the balance.

Although Cecil was a left-handed power hitter, the biggest hit of his career would now come from a pitch that he reached out and stroked to left field. The ball dropped in front of the charging Brian Downing, and two runs crossed the plate.

The Angels hadn't trailed in the Series, and they hadn't trailed in this final game until now. They were down 4 to 3 as they batted in the eighth.

Marshall Edwards went to center field as a defensive replacement for Gorman Thomas, who was hampered by a bad knee. Don Baylor lifted a deep fly ball in that direction, but Edwards made a great leaping catch against the fence to take away the extra-base bid.

The Californians still had a positive attitude, since the Brewers couldn't use their closer, Rollie Fingers. The bullpen ace had a muscle tear in his throwing arm.

Kuenn then beckoned rookie Peter Ladd, who closed out the Angel season with his second save, leaving a frustrated Reggie Jackson on deck. In his first season in California after starring with the Yankees, Reggie was disappointed that he wouldn't have a chance to hit all those World Series homers this year as he had done in New York.

Instead Milwaukee earned the right to co-host a third World Series, but for the first time in the American League. The Brewers won the ALCS not because of their prolific hitting, but because of a sounder defense and better employment of the fundamentals.

In addition to Edwards' sterling catch, Moore, a former catcher now converted to the outfield, made a perfect throw to third base after Fred Lynn's third hit in the fifth inning. He cut down Jackson as he was trying to go from first to third. After both Edwards' and Moore's fielding gems, the next batter followed with a hit, so these heads-up plays saved two runs.

Conversely, when the Brewers scored their first run in the opening inning, a bad throw from third base by Doug DeCinces set up a runner at third. Ted Simmons' sac fly would have just become the third out if not for this costly miscue.

Angel manager Gene Mauch was no stranger to seeing one of his teams blow a sure thing. His 1964 Phillies had a six-game lead in the National League with a week to go and lost out to the Cardinals on the final day of the season.

The Milwaukee fans had been devastated when the National League Braves defected to Atlanta for Ted Turner's TV money. The Brewers filled the void for baseball-starved fans in Wisconsin. They had forgotten the Braves and now had another fine team in another league to root for, and certainly to be proud of.

BREWERS-ANGELS RECAP

	R	H	E
Milwaukee	4	6	0
California	3	11	4

Winning pitcher- McClure
Losing pitcher- Sanchez
Save- Ladd
Home run- Oglivie

HEROES *** Moore, Cooper, Edwards
GOATS << DeCinces, Jackson

1983

MAJOR HEADLINES

President Reagan signs a bipartisan bill designed to rescue Social Security from bankruptcy.

Sally Ride becomes the first woman to travel in space with the space shuttle Challenger.

A suicide bomb explodes in Lebanon at a Marine barracks in Beirut. The explosion kills 241 U.S. marines and sailors, who were members of a peacekeeping force.

American troops invade Grenada to rescue American citizens, whose safety was being threatened by a Grenadian militia and Cuban partisans.

SPORTS

Baseball: Baltimore beats Philadelphia in a five-game World Series.

Pro Football: Washington defeats Miami in Super Bowl XVII. ('82 Season)

College Football: University of Miami wins the National Championship.

Pro Basketball: Philadelphia beats Los Angeles in NBA finals.

College Basketball: North Carolina State defeats Houston at the buzzer in NCAA final.

Hockey: NY Islanders take fourth straight Stanley Cup by defeating Edmonton in finals.

U.S. Open Tennis-
    Men's Finals: Jimmy Connors defeats Ivan Lendle.
    Women's Finals: Martina Navratilova defeats Chris Evert Lloyd.

MOVIES- ACADEMY AWARDS

Best Actor: Robert Duvall, *Tender Mercies*
Best Actress: Shirley MacLaine, *Terms of Endearment*
Best Director: James L. Brooks, *Terms of Endearment*
Best Picture: *Terms of Endearment*

CHAPTER XXXVIII
DARN THOSE WHITE SOX

Saturday, October 8, 1983- Comiskey Park,, Chicago, IL
American League Championship Series, Game Four
Baltimore Orioles 3, Chicago White Sox 0 (10 innings)

The Chicago White Sox picked the worst time to have their first major batting slump of the 1983 season. The Chisox had romped in the American League West, winning the title by twenty games. They led the majors in wins and runs scored, and were therefore the favorites over the East Champion Baltimore Orioles in the American League Championship Series. Chicago hoped to win its first pennant since 1959, and only their second AL flag in sixty-four years. Fans in the Windy City finally had someone to root for other than the Bears.

After winning the opener behind eventual Cy Young hurler LaMarr Hoyt, the Pale Hose could only manage to score one run in their next two losses to Baltimore. As they prepared for Game Four in front of the home fans at the old ball park on the South Side, Comiskey Park, they knew they had to relocate their bats, or their hopes to extend an outstanding season would end.

The game moved along rapidly with neither team mounting a scoring threat. Southpaw Britt Burns was the White Sox' number four starter, but today he was looking like Sandy Koufax. The Orioles started Storm Davis, but his mound work was limited to six innings, when another lefty, Tippy Martinez, assumed the controls.

The Sox, who averaged over five runs a game during the regular campaign, were still seeking their first run of this game as they batted in a scoreless seventh inning.

Manager Tony LaRussa had made a move that would cost his squad a run, and possibly the chance to play a fifth game the next day. He replaced his regular shortstop, Scott Fletcher, with backup Jerry Dybzinski. Fletcher had gone hitless in the first three games, thus LaRussa would try anything to rekindle his offense.

Chicago had its best scoring opportunity in the seventh inning. The White Sox put two men on third base- the only thing wrong was that they were both there at the same time.

Dybzinski came up with two on and bunted into a force out at third. Then, when Julio Cruz singled, Dybzinski raced full-force around second base and headed for third. Running with his head down, the beleaguered shortstop almost ran into the lead runner, Vance Law. Third-base coach Jim Leyland held Law at third on the hard-hit ball.

As the play trapped both runners, Law finally streaked for home, but second-baseman Rick Dauer nailed him at the plate. Law slammed into the catcher, Rick Dempsey, but the Oriole receiver bravely held on to the ball and tagged out the runner. The play, which could have made any blooper highlight film, aborted the Sox' scoring bid.

The White Sox did manage to get two men on with two out in the ninth, but their other Law, Rudy, ended the threat by striking out.

Burns had pitched nine strong innings for the Chisox. Although his pitch count had reached 149, LaRussa gave him a vote of confidence by leaving him in to start the tenth inning.

Unfortunately for Burns, pitch number 150 was one too many. Tito Landrum, a seldom-used outfielder, crushed that pitch into the upper deck in left to break the scoreless tie.

Landrum was not even on the Oriole roster until August 30. The twenty-eight-year-old rookie had spent most of his career in the St. Louis Cardinal farm system, but came to Baltimore as a throw-in from a prior trade with the Cards.

Landrum was on the Oriole club because management wanted to go with an extra batter and one less pitcher in the postseason. In a contrasting experience, he was preparing to go to the Little World Series with Louisville but instead got the call from a team that was about to go to the Big Show. Tito couldn't have dreamed that it would be his homerun that would send him to the World Series. Hollywood couldn't have written a more credible script.

The icing on the pennant-winning cake was sprayed on by fellow teammates Cal Ripken, Eddie Murray, Gary Roenicke, and Benny Ayala. The first three singled, and Ayala's long sac fly capped the three-run inning.

Martinez finished a fine four innings of labor to receive credit for the 3-0 verdict. The Birds won their sixth pennant and first under their rookie manager, Joe Altobelli. Altobelli succeeded the legendary Earl Weaver, who had had a long and successful career as the Oriole skipper before retiring after the 1982 season.

The Chicagoans won ninety-nine games during the regular season with a blend of solid power and excellent front-line pitching. However, the White Sox offense suffered a power outage in the LCS. They scored only three runs in the four games.

White Sox followers had to wait forty years between the club's last two pennants and another twenty-four years for their latest postseason trip. They now wondered if they would have to wait another generation for the team's next October appearance.

ORIOLES-WHITE SOX RECAP

	R	H	E
Baltimore	3	9	0
Chisox	0	10	0

Winning pitcher- T. Martinez
Losing pitcher- Burns
Home run- Landrum

HEROES ** T. Martinez, Landrum
GOAT < Dybzinki

1984

MAJOR HEADLINES

Great Britain and the Peoples' Republic of China reach an agreement to return Hong Kong to Chinese rule in 1997.

India's four-time Prime Minister, Indira Gandhi, is assassinated.

In North Carolina, Margie Velma Barfield becomes the first woman to be executed for a Capital crime in the United States since 1962.

Geraldine Ferrara becomes the first woman to run on a presidential ticket as vice presidential candidate with Walter Mondale. The pair are walloped by incumbent President Reagan in the November election.

SPORTS

Baseball: Detroit Tigers defeat the San Diego Padres in a five-game World Series.

Pro Football: The LA Raiders impressively defeat Washington in Super Bowl XVIII. ('83 Season)

College Football: Brigham Young is voted the National Champion.

Pro Basketball: Boston beats Los Angeles in the NBA finals.

College Basketball: Georgetown edges Houston in the NCAA final.

Hockey: Edmonton dethrones four-time champion Islanders in the Stanley Cup finals.

U.S. Open Tennis-
    Men's Finals: John McEnroe defeats Ivan Lendl.
    Women's Finals: Martina Navratilova defeats Chris Evert Lloyd.

MOVIES- ACADEMY AWARDS

Best Actor: F. Murray Abraham, *Amadeus*
Best Actress: Sally Field, *Places in the Heart*
Best Director: Milos Forman, *Amadeus*
Best Picture: *Amadeus*

CHAPTER XXXIX
FLUBS OF THE CUBS

Sunday, October 7, 1984- Jack Murphy Stadium, San Diego, CA
National League Championship Series, Game Five
San Diego Padres 6, Chicago Cubs 3

The baseball season in the city of Chicago rarely lasts into the fall. Like the lyrics to the song, "*Autumn Leaves*," for fans in the Windy City, "The days grow short when you reach September."

For this reason, the Second City was decidedly excited for the second straight year. Chicago would again have postseason action. Instead of the White Sox, this time it was the Cubs.

With the best record in the National League in 1984, the Eastern champs were favored to beat their Western rivals, the San Diego Padres, and earn a World Series berth for the first time since 1945. The Padres, another former expansion team in only its sixteenth year of operation, featured all-stars Steve Garvey, Tony Gwynn, Graig Nettles, and Rich "Goose" Gossage.

However, San Diego had one of the worst groups of pitchers ever to appear in Autumn. Gossage, the former Yankee fireballer, picked up a Metro Pass for his expected daily commute between the bullpen and the pitcher's mound.

The playoff had opened in Chicago, and in the two games at Wrigley Field, the Cubbies almost annihilated their opponents. The Pads, though, managed to take the first postseason contest ever played in San Diego.

The fourth game was a chiller. When Padre first-basemen Garvey belted a ninth-inning homer, the two rivals prepared for another tie-breaking skirmish on a sunny Sunday afternoon at Jack Murphy Stadium. Nobody could imagine a better setting for a game of this magnitude than this picturesque Southern California city with the near-perfect climate.

The Cubs not only had their best pitcher working the game for the pennant, but also the major leagues' most effective hurler in '84. Rick Sutcliffe had a 17-1 record since coming over from Cleveland in June, including a 13-0 whitewashing in the NLCS opener. He had a fifteen-game winning steak and had not tasted defeat since June 29.

The Padre starter, Eric Show, looked like he forgot when batting practice ended and the game began. First-baseman Leon "Bull" Durham and backstop Jody Davis took him deep in the first two innings for a huge 3 to 0 lead. After he walked Sutcliffe, manager Dick Williams had seen enough and began his bullpen parade.

Williams had won four pennants and three World Series in the American League with Boston and Oakland, and was now hoping to win his first title in the Senior Circuit. Surprisingly, his relievers stopped the Cubs from scoring more runs and gave the home team an opportunity to get back into the game.

With their Cy Young ace on the mound, Cub fans were more optimistic with each inning that they would soon be celebrating their first pennant in thirty-nine years. Although Sutcliffe loaded the bases with nobody out in the sixth, San Diego could only manage two long outfield fly balls to tally their first two runs.

As the Padres prepared to take their turn at bat in the seventh inning, Chicago led by a slim 3-2 count with only nine outs to go for the flag. For Cub followers, the San Diego seventh will remain a horrific memory of one of the worst disasters that city has suffered since the Chicago Fire.

Sutcliffe had shown in the sixth that he might be slightly tiring, but the Cubs were involved in their biggest game since the end of World War Two. Manager Jim Frey was sticking with his ace, who had brought the club this far, until he could no longer pitch.

Carmelo Martinez led off for San Diego by drawing a walk and then reached second on a bunt sacrifice. The demons that had prevented the Boston Red Sox from hoisting a World Championship banner since 1918 were apparently doing double duty in this encounter. Tim Flannery then hit a ground ball to first. The steady-fielding Durham moved over to pick up the ball, but to the horror of the Cubs and their supporters, it skipped under his glove for an error. As the ball trickled into right field, Martinez crossed the plate with the tying run.

The Cub nightmare was not yet finished. Alan Wiggins singled Flannery to second, bringing up one of baseball's top hitters, Tony Gwynn. Tony smacked another hard shot toward second base that could have been a double play.

Instead the ball took a bad hop that would have been déjà vu to Tony Kubek. It bounced high over Ryne Sandberg's head, found a gap in right-center field, and became a two-run double. The pesky Steve Garvey, who would earn MVP honors for this five-game clash, followed with a single for the fourth run of the inning. With that hit, Garvey effectively put a lid on Rick Sutcliffe's magnificent season.

With a 6 to 3 lead, the Padres did what the Yankees had done for several seasons. They brought in Gossage to preserve the advantage and close out the game. This would not, however, be a routine save. It became the save that brought the first pennant to San Diego.

The Pads had become only the second team to bounce back and win a League Championship Series after losing the first two games. They were the first NL club to accomplish this feat, duplicating the Milwaukee Brewers in the American League in the 1982 season.

For the second consecutive year, a Chicago baseball team had had an excellent season, but came up short in the League Championship Playoff. The Cubs were wondering when they would make the Final Four again. The pain of finishing second wouldn't be so bad if it didn't take another forty years to earn a chance to be first again.

PADRES-CUBS RECAP

	R	H	E
San Diego	6	8	0
Chi Cubs	3	5	1

Winning pitcher- Lefferts
Losing pitcher- Sutcliffe
Home runs- Durham, J. Davis

HERO * Gwynn
GOAT < Durham

1985

MAJOR HEADLINES

New York subway gunman Bernard Goetz is indicted on a minor illegal weapons possession charge.

A major earthquake strikes Mexico City killing thousands and causing heavy property losses.

Palestinian terrorists hijack the Italian cruise liner, Achille Lauro. A wheelchair-bound American tourist, Leon Klinghoffer, is shot and killed and thrown overboard by the hijackers.

President Reagan and Soviet Premier Mikhail Gorbachev attend a Summit meeting in Geneva, Switzerland.

Pete Rose shatters Ty Cobb's career hit record in major league baseball.

SPORTS

Baseball: Kansas City Royals surprise St. Louis to win all-Missouri World Series.

Pro Football: San Francisco beats Miami in Super Bowl XIX. ('84 Season)

College Football: Oklahoma is voted the National Champion.

Pro Basketball: Los Angeles defeats Boston in the NBA finals.

College Basketball: Villanova upsets Georgetown to win the NCAA championship.

Hockey: Edmonton repeats as Stanley Cup champion by whipping Philadelphia in finals.

U.S. Open Tennis-
    Men's Finals: Ivan Lendl beats John McEnroe.
    Women's Finals: Hana Mandlikova beats Martina Navratilova.

MOVIES- ACADEMY AWARDS

Best Actor: William Hurt, *Kiss of the Spider Woman*
Best Actress: Geraldine Page, *The Trip to Bountiful*
Best Director: Sydney Pollack, *Out of Africa*
Best Picture: *Out of Africa*

CHAPTER XL
OUT OF THE PARK WITH CLARK

Wednesday, October 17, 1985- Dodger Stadium, Los Angeles, CA
National League Championship Series, Game Six
St. Louis Cardinals 7, Los Angeles Dodgers 5

Once again it was a nerve-racking battle of East versus West in the 1985 National League finals. The eastern champs, the St. Louis Cardinals, invaded the West for a high-noon duel in the sun with their rivals, the Los Angeles Dodgers.

The home team triumphed in each of the first five games. The Cards had lost the first two in Los Angeles but bounced back to take the middle three in St. Louis. Since the Major League Board of Governors had voted to expand the League Finals to a best-of-seven as in the World Series, the Cardinals would need another victory to clinch the pennant, while the California club hoped to force a deciding seventh game. But first, both clubs would square off in Game Six under the brilliant blue skies of Dodger Stadium.

Today's game, like so many of the matches since the conception of the Divisional format sixteen years ago, would not produce a winner until the final inning, and a controversial managerial decision would play a big part in the outcome.

The Dodgers jumped off to a quick two-run lead, and when their hard-hitting third-baseman, Bill Madlock, smacked his third homer of the playoff series in the fifth inning, LA had a 4 to 1 lead. Madlock had driven in one of the first two runs, so he was using a smoking bat.

The Red Birds didn't want to have to play another game in enemy territory, so they mounted an offensive in the seventh inning, showing everyone why they won 101 games during the season. Darrel Porter and Tito Landrum, former Baltimore Oriole hero, led with singles, moved up on an infield out, and scored as the National League batting champion and MVP, Willie McGee, lined a hard single to center.

Dodger starter Orel Hershiser had been on cruise control through the first six, but he apparently had nothing left in the tank. Veteran manager Tommy Lasorda summoned his bullpen ace, Tom Niedenfuer, to stem the bleeding.

The first batter to face the reliever was shortshop Ozzie Smith. The defensive genius was not renowned for his hitting prowess, but not a soul could convince Niedenfuer of this fact. The Wizard of Ozzie had torched the hurler for a ninth-inning walk-off homer in the previous game at Busch Stadium to send the Series back to the West Coast with St. Louis leading for the first time.

This time, Ozzie failed to hit another home run, but he managed a wicked line drive into the right-field corner for three bases. The game was deadlocked, and the fielding whiz was also becoming a menace with the bat. When Ozzie Smith was at the plate, the Dodgers must have thought that Stan Musial had come out of retirement.

Cardinal skipper Whitey Herzog was at a slight disadvantage, since his club had lost its long-time bullpen leader, Bruce Sutter, to free agency. Herzog now used Todd Worrel in a spot formerly reserved for Sutter.

In the Dodger eighth, Mike Marshall greeted Worrel with a home run into the pavilion in left field. The partisan crowd screamed with joy. The Californians were three outs from forcing a seventh game they were confident they would then win.

But in order to capture a seventh game, the Dodgers would first have to take care of business here in Game Six. The annoying McGee stroked his third single with one out. When he stole second, the Dodgers were faced with the task of pitching to Smith once again. Niedenfuer worked a little too carefully to Ozzie and walked him. Tommy Herr then grounded out, advancing the runners to second and third.

The drama now produced the most controversial moment of the season. The next batter, Jack Clark, was the only legitimate power hitter on a Cardinal ball club that featured speed and timely hitting to all fields.

With first base open, manager Lasorda faced a major dilemma. Should he walk Clark, or should he elect to pitch to the slugger?

Back in the seventh inning when the Cards rallied for their three runs, Clark had struck out leaving two men on base. A rib injury had disabled him for more than a month, and since his return to the lineup in mid-September, he had not cleared the outfield fences even once.

Lasorda therefore decided to pitch to Clark but warned his reliever to be very careful not to give him anything good to hit. If a fastball over the plate is careful, then Niedenfuer followed instructions perfectly on his first delivery.

Clark swung, and everyone knew right away that the ball was out of the park. It landed half-way up the left-field bleachers for a three-run wallop. The Dodgers and the crowd both became sullen, as Clark's round-tripper gave the Cards a 7 to 5 lead, which they would hold on to for a stirring victory.

With the win, the Cardinals would go on to their fourteenth World Series. For the Dodgers, who had won their share of cliff-hangers, the defeat was devastating. They would return home for the winter, their splendid season now just a memory.

Lasorda has been asked many times why he eschewed walking Clark, and he always stands firm, defending his decision with a positive aplomb. Clark had not been hitting well since his return to the lineup, and Tommy elected to take his chances with the slumping hitter.

The next batter would be a dangerous left-hand hitter, Andy Van Slyke, and there weren't any dependable southpaws available in Lasorda's pen. Besides, creating a bases-loaded situation would leave no margin for error, should his pitcher walk the next batter. So Lasorda decided to pitch to Clark, and the rest is history.

Tom Lasorda spent his entire career in the Dodger organization, going all the way back to their days in Brooklyn, first as a pitcher, than as a coach, and finally the manager. Even though this one time, the results didn't go his way, he was one of the most successful and popular managers of all time. For his managerial skills and leadership, Tom Lasorda was quickly elected to the Baseball Hall of Fame in Cooperstown.

CARDINALS-DODGERS RECAP

	R	H	E
St. Louis	7	12	1
Los Angeles	5	8	0

Winning pitcher- Worrell
Losing pitcher- Niedenfuer
Save- Dayley
Home runs- Madlock, Marshall, J. Clark

HERO * J. Clark
GOAT < Niedenfuer

1986

MAJOR HEADLINES

The United States launches air strikes on Libyan terrorist bases.

The U.S. space shuttle Challenger explodes moments after liftoff. Six astronauts and a New Hampshire school teacher, Christa McAuliffe, perish on board the craft.

In California, noted actor Clint Eastwood is elected mayor of Carmel-by-the-Sea.

A major accident occurs at a Russian nuclear reactor plant in Chenobyl in the Ukraine. Thirty-one people are killed and significant quantities of radioactive material are spread over much of Europe.

A gala celebration for the 100th birthday of the Statue of Liberty includes fireworks, concerts, and a return of the tall ships to New York Harbor.

SPORTS

Baseball: New York Mets edge Boston in seven games in the World Series.

Pro Football: Chicago Bears wallop the New England Patriots in Super Bowl XX.
    ('85 Season)

College Football: Penn State wins the National Championship.

Pro Basketball: Boston defeats Houston for the NBA title.

College Basketball: Louisville defeats Duke in the NCAA final.

Hockey- Montreal over Calgary in Stanley Cup finals.

U.S. Open Tennis-
    Men's Finals: Ivan Lendl beats Miloslav Mecir.
    Women's Finals: Martina Navratilova beats Helena Sukova.

MOVIES- ACADEMY AWARDS

Best Actor: Paul Newman, *The Color of Money*
Best Actress: Marlie Matlin, *Children of a Lesser God*
Best Director: Oliver Stone, *Platoon*
Best Picture: *Platoon*

CHAPTER XLI
ANGELS WITH EGG ON THEIR FACES

Sunday, October 12, 1986- Anaheim Stadium, Anaheim, CA
American League Championship Series Game Five
Boston Red Sox 7, California Angels 6 (11 innings)

If there was ever any doubt that the Divisional playoffs were a good idea, Game Five of the American League Championship Series would dispel that doubt in 1986. The League Finals between the California Angels and the Boston Red Sox had more drama than a Shakespeare play, and the fifth game had more ups and down than an elevator.

This remarkable contest, played on a typically sunny Sunday afternoon in the Angels' home park just down the road from Disneyland, saw victory snatched from defeat and a goat turned into a hero. Only the improbable was probable.

The Red Sox, after splitting the opening pair in Boston, traveled cross-country to Southern California and blew leads in the previous two games, something with which fans in Beantown were well-acquainted. In the last encounter, their reliever, Calvin Schiraldi, walked in the tying run in the ninth inning in a game the Bosox would eventually lose in eleven.

The club trailed three-games to one, and another loss would give the Angels their first pennant in their twenty-six-year history. To make matters worse, the regular Boston center-fielder, Tony Armas, injured his ankle crashing into the wall in the second stanza. Armas was chasing a well-hit ball by Doug DeCinces that went for a double. Armas had to leave the game, and he was replaced by Dave Henderson, a reserve outfielder, whom the Sox had just acquired in a trade with Seattle in August.

Henderson soon had the opportunity to demonstrate Murphy's Law, where things that can get worse usually do. The Red Sox were leading 2 to 1 in the sixth inning, when, with one on, Henderson raced back to the fence for Bobby Grich's long drive. As he was about to snare the ball, he bounced into the wall. The impact loosened the ball from his glove and propelled it over the wall for a two-run home run.

The Anaheim fans and the national TV audience might have thought they were watching the Celtics and Lakers, but it was the Angels who were three innings short of a title. The Halos added two more markers in the seventh, and they entered the ninth inning with their best pitcher, Mike Witt, still on the mound.

With the Cal ace holding a convincing 5 to 2 lead, the stadium security force began to form a ring around the infield in anticipation of the final-out celebration. The guards remembered all-too well the experience in Yankee Stadium ten years ago, when Chris Chamblis had to fight his way around the bases after his ninth-inning home run that won the pennant. They wanted no repetition of that mob scene in the Bronx.

The Red Sox had suffered many heart-breaking losses in crucial games, but they never succumbed to defeat without a battle. Thus no one was surprised when their designated hitter, Don Baylor, came up with a man on and walloped a two-run homer. Everyone was accustomed to seeing a Bosox rally fall a run short, as in the momentous one-game playoff with the Yankees in 1978.

With two out, the security detail remained on the field, as an Angel pennant still loomed only moments away. When reliever Gary Lucas hit catcher Rich Gedman, Dave Henderson became the last Boston hope. The beleaguered outfielder didn't want to be the Bosox' last out of the season, especially after contributing to the California advantage.

Henderson was facing the Angels' closer, Donnie Moore. With a 2-2 count, he showed patience by fouling off several pitches he didn't like. Henderson finally found one to his liking and belted it over the left-center field wall. Suddenly the Angel lead was gone, and the shocked security guards removed themselves from the field.

The Boston rally gave them a 6 to 5 lead, postponed the Angels' pennant celebration, and left them with egg on their faces. It was California that now had to fight from behind.

That's just what they did in their half of the ninth. Rob Wilfong delivered the tying run with a single to right that scored Gary Pettis from second base. Wilfong hit the ball so hard that Pettis barely beat the throw and slid under Gedman's tag.

Once again the Angels roused the crowd, as they loaded the bases with only one out. The pennant in Southern California was now only ninety feet away. Steve Crawford, the fourth Red Sox pitcher, bore down, though, and retired DeCinces on a shallow fly to right and Grich on a soft tap to the mound.

With all the bounces, the game was taking on the appearance of a tennis match. Boston placed runners at the corners in the tenth inning, as the dangerous Jim Rice strode to the plate. Rice, one of baseball's most prolific batters, hit one hard, but it couldn't find a hole. The grounder went for a double play, and the Californians still had a shot.

The Anaheim crew couldn't mount a threat in the bottom of the tenth, and when the Bostonians loaded the bases in the top of the eleventh, up stepped the omnipresent Dave Henderson. This time Henderson lofted a deep fly ball to the outfield. The sacrifice fly produced the lead run.

Schiraldi, the relief pitcher who blew the previous game, this time retired the Angels in the bottom of the inning. He thus preserved an implausible 7-6 victory.

The Red Sox, who usually managed to lose games they expected to win, pulled one out in most dramatic fashion. Dave Henderson, who started the game on the bench, quickly went from goat to hero and helped shorten the Boston winter. Red Sox fans would have to wait until the World Series before finally experiencing the heartbreak they knew would eventually come.

RED SOX-ANGELS RECAP

	R	H	E
Boston	7	12	0
California	6	13	0

Winning pitcher- Crawford
Losing pitcher- Moore
Home runs- Gedman, Boone, Grich, Baylor, Henderson

HERO * Henderson
GOAT < Moore

CHAPTER XLII
METS HARD AS NAILS

Wednesday, October 15, 1986- Houston Astrodome, Houston, TX
National League Championship Series Game Six
New York Mets 7, Houston Astros 6 (16 innings)

After the 1986 American League playoff thriller in Anaheim, the National League wanted equal time in selling the Divisional Championship system to the public. Just when it appeared that no game could equal the Red Sox-Angels classic in Game Six, the New York Mets and Houston Astros staged one of the most incredible battles in postseason history. The National League rivals squared off in the sixth game of the NLCS at the major leagues' first indoor mecca, the Astrodome, in Houston.

The '86 Mets won 108 regular-season games, the third most winning total in National League history. For all their six-month success, the Mets would consider 1986 a failure if they didn't bring home a World Series banner.

The first piece of business for the New Yorkers was to turn back the Western Champion Houston Astros. The Astros were providing much tougher opposition than their Eastern rivals, whom the Mets trampled. The closest team to New York was the Phillies, who finished a distant twenty lengths behind.

With a tenuous three-game to two advantage, the Mets were almost desperate to win the sixth match. A loss would mean facing their nemesis, right-handed starter Mike Scott, in a seventh-game showdown before a hostile crowd on the road. Manager Davey Johnson wished to avoid this scenario at all possible cost.

Scott was the Senior Circuit's earned-run average leader and had throttled the Mets, allowing only one run while winning two complete-game starts. Houston felt certain that, if they could get past this game, the state of Texas would host its first World Series.

It didn't take long for gloom to descend on the Metropolitans and their sullen supporters. Before you could say, "Mike Scott," the Astros had three runs in their first turn at bat. Bill Doran singled, Denny Walling doubled, Glen Davis singled, Kevin Bass walked, and Jose Cruz singled. Left-hander Bob Ojeda, an eighteen-game winner, who also won his first start in the Championship round, was one or two batters from receiving the hook.

As sometimes happens when a pitcher gets rocked at the start, Ojeda overcame his early failure. The Astros didn't score any more runs through the next eight innings.

Houston manager Hal Lanier gave the ball to another lefty, Bob Knepper, who was equally formidable. Knepper had whipped the Mets three times without a loss during the season, and it appeared that he was about to conquer his Queens opponents for a fourth time.

Knepper still had the Mets shut out with only two hits as they came up for the last chance in the ninth inning. Lenny Dykstra, the fiery center-fielder known as "Nails" because of his hard play, came up as a pinch hitter. Dykstra, a left-handed batter, was not in the starting lineup against the tough lefty hurler.

Lenny won Game Three with a ninth-inning homer, and he now woke up his club with a booming triple to deep center field. Dykstra's three-bagger was the catalyst that brought the fading Mets back to life. Mookie Wilson singled, Keith Hernandez doubled, and the Flushing crew was a run short of tying the score.

Houston's top reliever, Dave Smith, who saved thirty-three wins during the season, entered the contest but lost sight of home plate. Smith walked power hitters Gary Carter and Darryl Strawberry, and when Ray Knight stroked a sacrifice fly to right, the score became knotted.

The Astros had a habit of playing extra-inning games in playoffs, and this habit now continued. Roger McDowell, the Mets' right-handed bullpen ace, kept Houston scoreless for the next five innings, while the New Yorkers could do no further damage until the fourteenth frame. The Mets broke through for a run, as Carter singled, Strawberry walked, and the scrappy second-baseman, Wally Backman, drove in the go-ahead run with a hard single to right.

The relentless Astros refused to lose. Just as the Mets thought they had finally wrapped up the flag, Astro center-fielder Billy Hatcher lined a bullet that just landed inside the left-field foul pole. Alas, the game would continue.

Dinners would have to wait. Few were leaving the ballpark, and the action also kept millions of fans glued to their TV sets. The adversaries struggled into the sixteenth inning before they would finally render a decision.

Strawberry doubled, and Knight's hit once again drove in the lead run for New York. Backman's walk preceded a wild pitch, before the dynamic Len Dykstra capped the rally with a two-run single.

The Mets took a 7-4 lead into the bottom half of the sixteenth but still didn't feel secure. After McDowell had ably done his job, Johnson entrusted the other half of his bullpen duo, lefty Jesse Orosco, with the task of tidying up and allowing all of the hungry customers to finally go home and eat.

Orosco, however, created trouble for himself in the Houston sixteenth, which was his third inning of labor. He started by walking the leadoff man, Davey Lopez.

The stubborn Texans were not yet conceding, and when Doran, Hatcher, and Davis all followed with hits, the Met lead was back down to a single run. Davey Johnson had exhausted his bullpen, and, as he had so often done, he prepared himself to sink or swim with his southpaw closer.

Kevin Bass, the dangerous right-fielder, was at bat with the tying run on third and the winner on first. Bass was a switch-hitter, so it didn't matter to him from which hand the opposition delivered the pitches.

Orosco had brought about his own problems by throwing fastballs to the Astros' contact hitters. To avoid paying the ultimate penalty of blowing this vital contest, he received instructions from backstop Carter not to throw anything but breaking balls. Thus, after a long at-bat, Bass finally struck out, ending the five-hour marathon.

The Houston fans, who had seen their heroes fall short after a classic struggle against the Phillies in the 1980 NLCS, now witnessed another near-miss in this Series. As they had done in 1980, they stood up and vigorously applauded both clubs for rewarding them with some of the most exciting baseball they had ever witnessed.

The New York Mets, who won their division with ease, had just survived the battle of their lives to win their third National League Championship Series in as many attempts. They didn't realize that they were about have an even bigger test for survival, when they would meet the Boston Red Sox in the upcoming World Series.

METS-ASTROS RECAP

	R	H	E
NY Mets	7	11	0
Houston	6	11	1

Winning pitcher- Orasco
Losing pitcher- Lopez
Home run- Hatcher

HEROES *** Dykstra, McDowell, Orasco
GOAT < Bass

CHAPTER XLIII
HOLD THE CHAMPAGNE—IT'S THE RED SOX

Saturday, October 25, 1986- Shea Stadium, Flushing, NY
World Series Game Six, New York Mets 6, Boston Red Sox 5 (10 innings)

If the New York Mets thought the Houston Astros were a tough act in the National League playoff, they had no idea how hard a test they would have in the 1986 World Series. After winning the NL East by twenty games and struggling past the Astros in six troublesome games, they had only to defeat the American League Champion Boston Red Sox to fulfill their season-long quest to win the World Championship.

The Red Sox, however, had other plans. The Sox took the first two on the road at Shea Stadium before the Mets evened the count in Bean town. The Bosox won the fifth game, and when both clubs returned to Queens, Boston had a chance to do something they hadn't done in sixty-eight years, win the World Series.

Red Sox manager John McNamara started the major league's top pitcher, twenty-five-game winner Roger Clemens, in Game Six in hopes of wrapping up the title. Davey Johnson, the Met skipper, countered with his ace southpaw, Bobby Ojeda.

The sixth game, played on a cool Saturday night at the Big Shea, was a microcosm of the whole Series. The Mets never led in the October Classic and never led in this game. They trailed by two runs, tied it, and then fell behind again 3 to 2.

The Flushing crew again knotted the contest in the eighth inning, and after nine rounds, this tense struggle remained deadlocked. It seemed like extra innings was becoming a tradition in the fantastic postseason of 1986.

Reliever Rick Aguilera faced the Red Sox as they batted in the tenth frame. Dave Henderson, the star of the ALCS, who saved Boston's season with his last-ditch heroics, greeted Aguilera by lining a home run off the left-field scoreboard. Two batters later, the Sox' hitting machine, Wade Boggs, doubled, and when Marty Barrett singled him home, the gloom that descended over Shea Stadium was more dense than the fog that enveloped the field throughout the game.

New York came up in the home tenth trailing 5 to 3, and some of the fans even started for the exits. Loyal Met fanatics could not bear to see the greatest season in their team's history end in such ignominious defeat.

Calvin Schiraldi, the hurler who won the critical fifth AL playoff game against the Angels, was on the mound, and he quickly retired the first two batters. The last hope for the New Yorkers was catcher Gary Carter.

As Schiraldi drew ahead by two strikes, the electronic scoreboard flashed a sign, "Congratulations, Red Sox." The television cameramen had stationed themselves inside the Bosox clubhouse to capture the frenetic celebration that would soon begin.

The Media, consisting of announcers, reporters, photographers, and the waiting cameramen, descended on the clubhouse like a swarm of bees to catch the spirit of a startling and major sports upset. The TV graphics from NBC proclaimed that this would be the first World Series victory for the Boston Red Sox since 1918.

Against this backdrop, cases of champagne remained sealed, waiting for an overjoyed crew of players to consume them. In moments the new champs would open them. Carter, however, delayed the party as he lined a single to left. The next batter was the versatile rookie, Kevin Mitchell, who played every position but pitcher and catcher during the season. Mitchell followed with another hit, and those who were leaving the ballpark remained in the aisles; maybe the baseball season was not quite over yet.

With the potential tying runs aboard, third-baseman Ray Knight strode to the plate. Knight didn't want to be the one who ended the Met season, since his costly seventh-inning error led to a Boston run.

Again the hitter was in a two-strike hole, but he finally blooped one into center, driving in Carter and sending Mitchell to third. Tension started to show on McNamara's band, as the manager brought in Bob Stanley in hopes of finally ending the suffering.

Up stepped the likable Mookie Wilson to try to keep the dream alive. Mookie would have one of the great World Series at-bats without earning a hit.

Wilson fouled off several pitches, but it was the fateful seventh pitch that revived the Mets and emptied the Red Sox clubhouse. Stanley tried to throw a high, inside fastball that sailed over catcher Rich Gedman's head. On the wild pitch, Mitchell scored the tying run, and Knight raced to third.

The errant delivery almost hit Mookie, but he nimbly leaned out of the way to avoid being struck by the ball. That action would only load the bases and enable the Bosox to still win the game, set, and match if they retired the next batter. Now the pressure of losing was gone, and the possible winning run stood at second base.

It seemed like forever that Wilson remained in the batter's box, but he finally swung at Stanley's tenth offering and stroked a fair ground ball toward first base. The inning would end, and the game would continue.

First-baseman Bill Buckner moved into position to field the grounder. But for whatever reason, whether it was Buckner's ailing legs or Babe Ruth's ghost blocking his path, the ball trickled through his legs and into right field. Knight trotted across the plate with the winning run, as the Red Sox looked on in a catatonic-like shock.

The New York Mets had made one of the most improbable comebacks in sports history to take a stunning 6-5 decision. The hex on the Boston team, which had last triumphed in the Fall Classic during World War One, remained for at least another day. Instead of flying home in triumph, the defeat would force the Red Sox to remain in New York and play another seventh game.

The Sox, who were one strike away from losing the American League playoff, were one strike away from winning the World Series. The same agony that suffocated the California Angels now engulfed the Boston Red Sox and their long-suffering followers all over New England.

Although Bill Buckner was the culprit in defeat, the manager had to assume part of the blame for this disastrous loss. McNamara knew Buckner's bad wheels might not hold up for nine innings or longer. Instead of providing a defensive replacement in the tenth inning, he kept his star in the game with tragic results.

McNamara later tried to justify his decision, stating that Buckner had good hands. For the Boston Red Sox, it was a shame the manager didn't also notice his feet.

The name of Bill Buckner would add to a growing list of other Boston anti-heroes like Enos Slaughter, Johnny Lindell, Bucky Dent, and in this game, Bob Stanley, whose names would forever live in infamy among Red Sox fans. The champagne in the clubhouse remained unopened for at least another day, or perhaps an indeterminable length of time.

The long-time radio voice of the New York Mets, Bob Murphy, always ended his description of each Met win with the comment, "We'll be right back with the happy recap." When the club would lose, Murphy omitted the word "happy." That extra word was a late and unexpected addition to his narration in this broadcast. Would anyone care to guess what type of a recap would follow the seventh game?

METS-RED SOX RECAP

	R	H	E
Mets	6	8	2
Boston	5	13	3

Winning pitcher- Aguilera
Losing pitcher- Schiraldi
Home run- Henderson

HERO * Wilson
GOATS << Stanley, Buckner

1987

MAJOR HEADLINES

President Reagan announces the first trillion-dollar budget.

Public hearings in the Senate and the House of Representatives are held to investigate the Iran-Contra affair. Lt. Colonel Oliver North testifies that all of his activities were authorized by his superiors, and President Reagan denies any knowledge of the diversion of funds to the Contras.

Wall Street suffers a major decline as the Dow plummets a record 508 points.

President Reagan and Soviet leader Gorbachev sign a major agreement to dismantle all American and Russian long-range missiles with a range of 300 to 3600 miles.

SPORTS

Baseball: Minnesota defeats St. Louis in seven games in the World Series.

Pro Football: The Giants wallop Denver in Super Bowl XXI. ('86 Season)

College Football: Miami wins the National Championship.

Pro Basketball: The Lakers defeat the Celtics in the NBA finals.

College Basketball: Indiana edges Syracuse in the NCAA final.

Hockey: Edmonton Beats Philadelphia in the Stanley Cup finals.

U.S. Open Tennis-
    Men's Finals: Ivan Lendl beats Mats Wilander.
    Women's Finals: Martina Navratilova beats Steffi Graf.

MOVIES- ACADEMY AWARDS

Best Actor: Michael Douglas, *Wall Street*
Best Actress: Cher, *Moonstruck*
Best Director: Bernardo Bertolucci, *The Last Emperor*
Best Picture: *The Last Emperor*

CHAPTER XLIV
VIOLA FIDDLES WITH CARDS

Sunday, October 25, 1987- Metrodome, Minneapolis, MN
World Series Game Seven, Minnesota Twins 4, St. Louis Cardinals 2

Although the deciding seventh-game site for the 1987 World Series was the home of the American League champion Minnesota Twins, their National League opponent Saint Louis Cardinals had a distinct advantage. Never in the eighty-four-year history of the Fall Classic had the home team won all the games.

The '87 Series was a "homer" Series, in that each club won all three games in its home park quite impressively. Series tradition indicated that the visiting Cardinals had a strong chance to take the seventh game and the Series, based on the history of this event.

What tradition didn't count on, though, was the intimidating Metrodome in Minneapolis, whose noise level from over-zealous Twins fans had given the Minnesotans the best home record in baseball. The Twins captured three-quarters of their home games and regarded visiting teams like hungry diners regard a buffet

Twins' ace lefty Frank Viola was making his third Series start, and the heavy work load made him look shaky early in the contest. The Cards reached Viola for four hits in the second inning to take a two-run lead.

Instead of upsetting the Red Birds, the crowd and the field seemed to inspire them. Left-fielder Vince Coleman made two outstanding throws to gun down Minnesota base runners attempting to score. In the second inning, he threw a strike to the plate nipping Don Baylor, who was trying to score on a single. Since the next batter, Steve Lombardozzi, produced a run-scoring safety, Coleman's stellar throw kept the Cardinals ahead.

In the fifth, Coleman again threw out another runner at the plate after Twins superstar Kirby Puckett had doubled in the tying run. The rotund, unlikely-looking All-star seemed to be the center piece of every Twin rally. If there was one player opposing teams did not wish to see up at the plate in a key situation, it was Kirby.

The Cardinals were playing an exceptionally alert defensive game, and when catcher Steve Lake briefly lost a delivery from pitcher Danny Cox, Puckett tried to advance to third base. Lake quickly retrieved the ball in the dirt and fired to third to nail Puckett on a play that would definitely make the TV highlight reel of "This Week in Baseball."

After his erratic start, Viola settled down, and this excellent seventh game was tied as the Twins batted in the home sixth. The tide started to turn, as the St. Louis hurlers loaded the bases on walks. Although the game was played indoors, Cardinal pitchers Cox and Todd Worrell appeared to be in a fog, losing site of the plate.

Shortstop Greg Gagne, who had scored the tying marker, now had a chance to give the Twins their first lead of the night. That he did, lining a hard smash down the third-base line. Third-sacker Tom Lawless tried to do his best Brooks Robinson imitation. He dove for the ball, picked it up, and fired to first, but he had no chance to get the speedy Gagne. This proved to be the hit that won the championship.

Minnesota scored an insurance run in the eighth, as left-fielder Dan Gladden drove in the club's fourth run with a double. Viola only allowed two hits after the second inning and retired eighteen of the last twenty batters he faced in his eight innings on the mound.

Although his starter appeared stronger as the game progressed, manager Tom Kelly still had one more weapon in his arsenal, and he insisted on using it. His closer, Jeff Reardon, was an invincible figure all season long, and now Kelly beckoned the bearded bullpen ace to lock up another win and the World Series.

Viola didn't feel the least bit tired, but he didn't mind letting Reardon finish the game, as he had done so many times during the long season and playoffs. Reardon responded by retiring the Cards in order to bring the first-ever World Championship title to the state of Minnesota.

For the first time in history, the home team won every game in a World Series. The Cardinals were formidable in Saint Louis, but, as they were all-year long, the Twins were practically unbeatable in the Metrodome.

The Twins had the lowest winning percentage of any team to ever win a World Series. Their .525 mark made it appear that Minnesota would offer only token resistance to any postseason opponent. The Twins, however, thrashed the Tigers in five games in the American League finals. They then benefited from the extra game with their wild, loud, homer-hankie-waving fans, pulling off an upset of major proportions. The World Championship was the club's first title since 1924, when the team was the Washington Senators.

Before the start of the Series, Red Bird manager Whitey Herzog, not known for his tact, offered an opinion that the Minnesota Twins were lucky to be playing in such a weak division as the AL West. He said that, if they had to compete in the Cardinals' NL East bracket, they would have been lucky to finish fifth.

The Twins didn't forget this ill-advised remark, and Herzog was left with a case of Foot-in-Mouth Disease. World Series MVP Frank Viola fiddled with the Cards, while Whitey Herzog turned up as a joker.

TWINS, CARDINALS RECAP

	R	H	E
Minnesota	4	10	0
St. Louis	2	6	0

Winning pitcher- Viola
Losing pitcher- Cox
Save- Reardon
Home runs- none

HEROES ** Viola, Reardon
GOAT << Cox, Worrell

1988

MAJOR HEADLINES

One of the worst droughts in more than fifty years causes the U.S. Government to designate much of the nation's agricultural counties as disaster areas.

A U.S. Navy missile fired from the Persian Gulf accidentally strikes and destroys an Iranian airliner, killing all 290 passengers aboard.

Vice President George Bush is elected president, defeating his Democratic opponent, Massachusetts Governor Michael Dukakis.

SPORTS

Baseball: The LA Dodgers upset Oakland in five games in the World Series.

Pro Football: Washington trounces Denver in Super Bowl XXII. ('87 Season)

College Football: Notre Dame convincingly wins the National Championship.

Pro Basketball: Los Angeles defeats the Detroit Pistons in the NBA finals.

College Basketball: Kansas defeats Oklahoma in the NCAA final.

Hockey: Edmonton defeats Boston in the Stanley Cup finals.

U.S. Open Tennis-
    Men's Finals: Mats Wilander defeats Ivan Lendl.
    Women's Finals: Steffi Graf defeats Gabriela Sabatini.

MOVIES- ACADEMY AWARDS

Best Actor: Dustin Hoffman, *Rain Man*
Best Actress: Jodie Foster, *The Accused*
Best Director: Barry Levinson, *Rain Man*
Best Picture: *Rain Man*

CHAPTER XLV
"I DON'T BELIEVE WHAT I JUST SAW"

Saturday, October 15, 1988- Dodger Stadium, Los Angeles, CA
World Series Game One, Los Angeles Dodgers 5, Oakland Athletics 4

The year 1988 was the fortieth anniversary of the memorable Truman-Dewey presidential election. Like that election, the pending World Series looked like a giant mismatch.

The Oakland Athletics were one of the toughest representatives the American League could offer in recent memory. Led by sluggers Jose Canseco and Mark McGwire, twenty-one-game winner Dave Stewart, and the major league's premier bullpen closer, Dennis Eckersley, the A's won 104 regular-season games and swept the Red Sox in the League Championship playoff.

The Los Angeles Dodgers staggered across the finish line, and then surprised everyone as they upset the heavily-favored Mets in the National League Championship. As they prepared for the opening game of the October Classic on a warm evening at scenic Dodger Stadium, Tommy Lasorda's crew was decimated by injuries.

The Dodgers' biggest problem was the apparent unavailability of their hitting star and team leader, Kirk Gibson. Gibson had carried the ball club on his bat all season, but a severely pulled left hamstring and badly injured right knee hampered the Dodger star. Gibby sat on the bench, but his status was doubtful.

Although LA took an early two-run lead on a Mickey Hatcher home run, their starting pitcher, Tim Belcher, was throwing like he had an early date and wanted to be excused. He escaped a bases-loaded jam in the first frame but committed the unpardonable sin of walking pitcher Stewart in the second.

For the second straight inning, Belcher wound up loading the bases, as Jose Canseco came to the plate. As Belcher faced the Oakland slugger, he must have felt like he was looking down the barrel of a shotgun.

Canseco didn't waste much time, rocketing a monster shot that dented one of the TV cameras stationed beyond the center-field fence.

The sixteenth grand slam homer in World Series competition appeared to launch the Athletics toward an inevitable title.

Dodger relievers Tim Leary and Brian Holton then did yeoman duty keeping the A's off the scoreboard, while the Hollywood club picked up a sixth-inning tally to draw within a run of the mighty Oakland warriors.

The Dodgers came up for their final at-bat in the ninth with a chance to tie or win the game, but their prognosis was grim. Stewart had done his job well, but Oakland manager Tony LaRussa made his customary call to the bullpen. Dennis Eckersley had saved forty-five games during the season, and there was no reason to believe the opposition would give him any trouble tonight.

True to form, Eckersley quickly retired the first two batters before pinch-hitter Mike Davis managed to draw a base-on-balls. Since it was now the pitcher's turn to hit, Lasorda needed another batter, but his depleted bench made him hard-pressed to find one.

Suddenly, out of the dugout stepped Kirk Gibson. The crowd stared in disbelief, then started to roar. For fans watching across the country on the tube, memories of a hobbled Willie Reed stepping onto the basketball court for the New York Knicks in the seventh game of the 1970 NBA finals started to form. Ironically the team that succumbed to Reed's Knicks was the club from Los Angeles, the Lakers.

Gibson staggered to the plate, and the crowd wondered how he would ever get to first base if he hit one. He looked to be in agony as he stood in the batter's box.

Eckersley worked slowly and deliberately, and Gibby fell behind by two strikes; only one more strike to go for the win. The hurler's concentration on Gibson was so intense that the fleet-footed Davis easily stole second base. If Kirk could somehow make contact and stroke the ball into the outfield, then the Dodgers would remain alive, and the game would continue.

Gibson fouled off several pitches and worked the count full to 3-2. Finally he swung and connected solidly. The ball quickly sailed into the right-field seats to give the Dodgers an implausible 5-4 victory.

The reaction was slow in coming, but, realizing what had just happened, manager Lasorda led his jubilant squad out of the dugout to await Kirk Gibson's arrival at home plate. Gibson pumped his fist in the air and slowly and triumphantly circled the bases.

Hall of Fame announcer Jack Buck was calling the game from the CBS radio booth. He echoed the sentiments of everyone who had just witnessed this memorable encounter, when he emotionally exclaimed, "I don't believe what I just saw!" What Buck had just seen was one of the most remarkable and heroic occurrences in the history of any sporting event.

Just as Willis Reed had inspired his Knickerbocker team with an unscheduled entrance into the starting lineup, so did Kirk Gibson energize his team with his unexpected appearance from the dugout.

Gibson made no further appearance in this World Series, but the demoralizing defeat caused unrepairable damage to the Athletics. Historians recalled Dusty Rhodes' startling homer in the 1954 Series, which started the Cleveland Indians on the way to a humiliating four-game whipping by the New York Giants.

Oakland likewise never recovered from Gibson's home run, as the Dodgers charged to a five-game triumph in one of the World Series' biggest upsets. Only a ninth-inning Mark McGwire home run in the third game prevented another sweep.

Just as Tom Dewey had been elected president until they counted the votes, the Oakland Athletics had won the World Series until they played the games.

DODGERS-ATHLETICS RECAP

	R	H	E
Los Angeles	5	7	0
Oakland	4	7	0

Winning pitcher- Pena
Losing pitcher- Eckersley
Home runs- Hatcher, Canseco, Gibson

HERO * Gibson
GOAT < Eckersley

1989

MAJOR HEADLINES

President Bush signs legislation designed to rescue the Savings and Loan industry.

The ship, Exxon Valdez, strikes an Alaskan reef, causing one of the largest oil spills in Unite States history.

President Bush nominates Army General Colin Powell as the first black Chairman of the Joint Chiefs of Staff.

A major earthquake strikes the San Francisco area just before the start of a World Series game at Candlestick Park. The quake causes sixty-two deaths.

U.S. troops invade Panama, overthrowing the government of Manuel Noriega, who is wanted on drug charges.

The collapse of the Communist regime is highlighted by the dismantling of the Berlin Wall, which had prevented residents of the Russian sector of the city from entering the American sector since 1961.

SPORTS

Baseball: Oakland sweeps the San Francisco Giants in Bay area World Series.

Pro Football: San Francisco edges Cincinnati in last-minute victory in Super Bowl XXIII. ('88 Season)

College Football: Miami University wins the National Championship.

Pro Basketball: Detroit defeats Los Angeles in the NBA finals.

College Basketball: Michigan wins controversial NCAA final from Seton Hall by one point in overtime.

Hockey: Calgary defeats Montreal in all-Canadian Stanley Cup finals.

U.S. Open Tennis:
    Men's Finals: Boris Becker beats Ivan Lendl.
    Women's Finals: Steffi Graf beats Martina Navratilova.

MOVIES- ACADEMY AWARDS

Best Actor: Daniel Day-Lewis, *My Left Foot*
Best Actress: Jessica Tandy, *Driving Miss Daisy*
Best Director: Oliver Stone, *Born on the Fourth of July*
Best Picture: *Driving Miss Daisy*

CHAPTER XLVI
WILL THE THRILL AND AMAZING GRACE

Monday, October 9, 1989- Candlestick Park, San Francisco, CA
National League Championship Series, Game Five
San Francisco Giants 3, Chicago Cubs 2

The contestants for the 1989 National League pennant had much in common. Both the San Francisco Giants and the Chicago Cubs had not been to the World Series in more than a generation. The Giants last won a pennant in 1962, losing by an eyelash to the Yankees in seven games. The Cubs hadn't been to the Big Show since 1945. The drought was about to end for one of these clubs.

In addition, both managers, Roger Craig for San Francisco and Don Zimmer for Chicago, had played on the 1955 Brooklyn Dodgers and 1962 New York Mets. Those Dodgers were the only club to ever win a World Series in Brooklyn, while the expansion New York Mets of '62 lost a record 120 games. They were one of the worst if not THE WORST major league team that ever took the field.

Finally the hitting stars of both squads were their outstanding first-basemen, Will (The Thrill) Clark of the Giants and Mark (Amazing) Grace of the Cubs. Both men were outstanding defensively at their position, and each was the top hitter of his team.

After splitting the first two contests in front of the ivy-covered walls of Wrigley Field, the adversaries returned to the City by the Bay for the next three. The Cubs held leads in the first two at Candlestick Park, which they were not able to maintain. This Monday matinee on a sunny San Francisco afternoon was therefore their last hope of breaking the World Series drought, which was now forty-four years and counting.

As they had done in the previous two games, the Cubs took an early lead in Game Five. In the third stanza, Giant left-fielder Kevin Mitchell lost a fly ball in the sun, as Jerome Walton raced to second on the error. All-star second-baseman Ryne Sandberg then delivered a run with a double.

That was all the Cubbies would get through the eight innings Giant starter Rick Reuschel was on the mound. It was not that the Cubs didn't have opportunities to nail Reuschel. The Giants simply helped him out with two double plays, and he pitched out of four first-and-third jams. The Windy City club just couldn't come up with the big hit when they needed it.

It seemed like the relentless Will Clark was involved in every Giant rally. Chicago starter Mike Bielecki nursed a 1 to 0, two-hit shutout as San Francisco batted in the seventh. Clark walloped a triple and scored the tying run on Mitchell's sacrifice fly.

The game turned in the Giant eighth, as Zimmer stayed too long with a tiring Bielecki. After he retired the first two batters, the righty promptly walked Candy Maldonado and Brett Butler and did give a damn. The skipper came out of the dugout, and everyone expected him to bring along the hook.

When the weary hurler told Zimmer he was all right, even Bielecki was surprised when the manager left him in the game. Bielecki then proceeded to walk Robby Thompson, and with the lefty Clark due up, southpaw Mitch Williams finally got the call.

Williams had saved thirty-six games for Zimmer's crew during the season. He went ahead by two strikes on the Giant slugger, but Clark hung in at 1-2. After fouling off several pitches, he drove a fast ball into center field for the hit that knocked in a pair of runs giving the Californians a 3 to 1 lead entering the ninth round.

Giant skipper Craig called for his closer, Steve Bedrosian, to finish the contest. Bedrosian retired the first two batters, but three W's, Wilkerson, Webster, and Walton all singled to draw the Windy City group a run closer at 3-2. Unfortunately for the Cubs, the W's did not also mean "win," as Sandberg grounded out. Mark Grace had already whacked two hits but wouldn't have another chance to bat. The Giants had struggled but finally won their first National League pennant in twenty-seven years.

Their reward would be an appointment with their rivals from across the bay, the Oakland Athletics. This would be the first time the World Series locale would be in one region since the Yankees and Brooklyn Dodgers squared off in 1956.

The Cubs seemed to be the National League clone of the Boston Red Sox. They lost the 1984 NL playoff after leading the Padres in the seventh inning of the deciding game, on an error at first base and a ground ball that bounced over second base for the winning run.

The Cubs had now lost their second National League playoff in as many attempts after blowing leads in each of the three Candlestick encounters. They had several chances to win the fifth game, but, like the Red Sox, their destiny appeared to be always finding a way to lose a game they needed to win.

Will Clark almost single-handedly won this series. Clark batted .650 in the five games, drove in eight runs, and belted thirteen hits including an extra-base barrage of three doubles, a triple, and two home runs. To Clark the ball must have looked like a beach ball as it floated up to the plate.

The ball must have looked almost as good to Mark Grace. Grace batted .647, with eleven hits that included three doubles, a triple, and a homer.

The NLCS was a showcase for these two fine first-basemen, but only Clark could move on to the World Series. The Giants would meet an Oakland clue that was still smarting from its stunning defeat at the hands of the Dodgers the previous season. With the A's looking to avenge that humiliation, the Giants would be in for a rough time in the October Classic.

The Cubs would go home for the forty-fifth straight winter without a pennant. If they wished to see the World Series, they would have to assume their customary position in front of their TV sets.

GIANTS-CUBS RECAP

	R	H	E
San Francisco	3	4	1
Chi Cubs	2	10	1

Winning pitcher- Reuschel
Losing pitcher- Bielecki
Save- Bedrosian
Home runs- none

HERO * Grace
GOAT < M. Williams

1990

MAJOR HEADLINES

President Bush signs into law legislation barring discrimination against the handicapped.

Operation Desert Shield forces arrive in Saudi Arabia to defend that country, after neighboring Kuwait is invaded by Iraq.

A major recession develops, causing massive layoffs and high unemployment.

The reunification of Germany, which had been divided between Allied and Communist control since the end of World War Two, is completed.

SPORTS

Baseball- Cincinnati completes a four-game sweep of Oakland in the World Series.

Pro Football: San Francisco 49ers repeat as NFL champs by walloping Denver in Super Bowl XXIV. ('89 Season)

College Football: Colorado and Georgia Tech share the National Championship..

Pro Basketball: Detroit beats Portland to repeat as NBA champs.

College Basketball: Nevada-Las Vegas (UNLV) wallops Duke in the NCAA final.

Hockey- Edmonton defeats Boston in the Stanley Cup finals.

U.S. Open Tennis-
    Men's Finals: Pete Sampras defeats Andre Agasse.
    Women's Finals: Gabriela Sabatini Defeats Steffi Graf

MOVIES- ACADEMY AWARDS

Best Actor: Jeremy Irons, *Reversal of Fortune*
Best Actress: Kathy Bates, *Misery*
Best Director: Kevin Costner, *Dances With Wolves*
Best Picture: *Dances With Wolves*

CHAPTER XLVII
A SAD NIGHT FOR ATHLETIC SUPPORTERS

Saturday, October 20, 1990- Oakland Coliseum, Oakland, CA
World Series Game Four, Cincinnati Reds 2, Oakland Athletics 1

The National League Champion Cincinnati Reds were on a World Series roll. In their last appearance in the Major League finals in 1976, they swept the New York Yankees in four straight.

As they prepared to battle the Oakland Athletics in the fourth game of the 1990 World Series at the Oakland Alameda County Coliseum, they were attempting to pull off their second straight Series sweep against the powerful A's.

Oakland was the defending World Champion, having taken four in a row from its rivals from across the bay, the San Francisco Giants, in 1989. Fans remembered that Series more for the two-week delay, when a frightening earthquake erupted just before the start of the third game at Candlestick Park, than for the games themselves.

The Athletics were overwhelming favorites in the '90 Series, but the Reds started strong and impressively won the first three matches. Cincinnati wanted to sweep, since a fifth game would still have to be played in Oakland, and the Red Men were afraid of how quickly momentum could turn the awesome Athletics around.

The Reds' urgency to win revealed itself in the first inning. They not only gave up a run on a Willie McGee double and Carney Landsford single, but lost their two top players, outfielders Billy Hatcher and Eric Davis, to injuries. The Reds didn't want to risk playing anymore games against their formidable opponents with a manpower shortage.

The Cincinnati starting hurler was Jose Rijo, who had shut down the Athletics in the opening game, limiting them to a run and two hits. After getting off to a rocky start in the first inning, the right-handed ace walked two men in the second, but then proceeded to pitch masterfully into the ninth inning. He retired the next twenty batters he faced before yielding to closer Randy Myers.

Meanwhile the Reds tried to put some runs on the board against the Oakland ace, Dave Stewart. You can't win if you don't score.

While Rios held the Oaks scoreless in a scintillating performance, Cincinnati finally broke through in their half of the eighth inning. They manufactured a pair of runs in an old-fashioned manner, applying the seldom-used art of the bunt in this era of millionaire, high-profile athletes.

After Barry Larkin led off with a single, Herm Winningham, with two strikes, crossed up the opposition with a well-placed bunt between home and third. He easily beat the throw of catcher Jamie Quirk to first base for another hit.

Heavy-hitting Paul O'Neil helped his club with another neat bunt that would have gone for a sacrifice, but Stewart's throw to first pulled second-baseman Willie Randolph, who was covering, off the bag for an error.

Now the bases were loaded, and after a fielder's choice tied the game, first-baseman Hal Morris provided the lead run with a sacrifice fly. The Reds now led 2 to 1 with an inning and a half to go.

The left-handed Myers was an excellent closer and did his job to perfection. He took over for Rios with one out in the ninth and retired the side to give the Cincinnati Reds their second straight World Series sweep. Rios easily earned the MVP award for his outstanding two pitching efforts.

The Reds won their fifth World Series title in nine appearances. For the second straight year, the losing team had worn the collar, and it was the fifteenth time the victors had won without losing a game.

The Oakland Athletics had just won their third consecutive American League pennant, but for the second time in three years, an underdog opponent from the Senior Circuit had upset them in the Fall showdown. The whitewash made for a sad night for Athletic supporters across Northern California.

The A's failed to contend mainly because they only played three-inning baseball, while the Reds played nine. Oakland scored a total of nine runs in the four games, but they all crossed the plate in the first three innings. The Athletics failed to score after the third inning of each game, and this lack of full-time productivity seldom leads to victory.

Reds' manager Lou Piniella, the former Yankee outfield star, did a masterful job of capturing the World Championship in his first year at the helm. After ending his fine playing career, Piniella first earned the opportunity to manage the Yankees. He had the misfortune, though, of working for meddling owner George Steinbrenner while failing to win a pennant. When the Reds finally rescued him from this distressing situation, Piniella showed everyone the poise and ability of a veteran manager, leading his club to an impressive victory.

Cincinnati had a dream season. They led from the opening day and never dropped out of first place. Their wire-to-wire finish reminded fans of the 1927 Yankees, the 1955 Brooklyn Dodgers, and the 1984 Detroit Tigers, although their World Series triumph surprised nearly everyone. Most people believed that, if the Series went only four games, Cincy would be the sweepees, not the sweepers.

Both the Reds and the Athletics have been involved in several more dramatic postseason games than the one just completed. None, however, was a more well-played and fast-paced contest than the one that concluded a titanic season in Cincinnati; the one that had the Reds sailing like kings of the world.

REDS-ATHLETICS RECAP

	R	H	E
Cincinnati	2	7	1
Oakland	1	2	1

Winning pitcher- Rijo
Losing pitcher- Stewart
Save- Myers
Home runs- none

HERO * Rijo
GOAT < Stewart

1991

MAJOR HEADLINES

The nation of Kuwait is liberated, as U.S. and Allied forces launch a devastating air and ground attack on Iraq in Operation Desert Storm.

A Congressional bank is ordered closed after revelations disclose that House members wrote 8331 bad checks.

The Senate approves the nomination of Clarence Thomas to the Supreme Court despite allegations of sexual harassment against him by former aide Anita Hill.

SPORTS

Baseball: Minnesota edges the Atlanta Braves in seven-game World Series.

Pro Football: Giants edge Buffalo by one point in Super Bowl XXV, ('90 Season), as the Bills miss a field goal on the final play of the game.

College Football: Miami and Washington share the National Championship.

Pro Basketball: The Chicago Bulls, led by Michael Jordan, win their first NBA title by beating the LA Lakers.

College Basketball: Duke defeats Kansas in the NCAA final.

Hockey: Pittsburgh defeats Minnesota in the Stanley Cup finals.

U.S. Open Tennis-
    Men's Finals: Stefan Edberg defeats Jim Courier.
    Women's Finals: Monica Seles defeats Martina Navratilova.

MOVIES- ACADEMY AWARDS

Best Actor: Anthony Hopkins, *The Silence of the Lambs*
Best Actress: Jody Foster, *The Silence of the Lambs*
Best Director: Jonathan Demme, *The Silence of the Lambs*
Best Picture: *The Silence of the Lambs*

CHAPTER XLVIII
BRAVES' BAD BASERUNNING BLUNDER

Sunday, October 27, 1991- Metrodome, Minneapolis, MN
World Series Game Seven, Minnesota Twins 1, Atlanta Braves 0 (10 innings)

What could be more remarkable than for a last-place team in one year rebounding to make it all the way to the World Series the following year? Simply, the answer is for two cellar-dwellers to get to the Big Show the next year.

The worst-to-first scenario occurred in the 1991 World Series. The Minnesota Twins, who won the whole ball of wax in 1987, slumped to last place in 1990 but were easily the best team in the American League in '91. They were convincing winners in the AL West and trounced Toronto in the League Championship Series.

Atlanta had been long-time doormats in the National League, but with an aggressive young team and an outstanding pitching staff headed by John Smoltz and Tommie Glavine, the Braves edged the Dodgers in the NL West, outlasted Pittsburgh in the playoffs, and won their first pennant since 1958, when the club played in Milwaukee.

In the Fall Classic, the Twins continued their home-field mastery as they had done in 1987. Their noisy, hanky-waving fans intimidated the opposition, and, after sweeping the first three home games at the Dome, the Minnesota entry had won seven straight there without a loss.

The Braves, on the other hand, won all of their contests in Atlanta and even had a chance to bring the trophy back to Dixie in Game Six. It took the future Hall-of-Famer, outfielder Kirby Puckett, to wreck their chances to become the first team to break serve. His walk-off home run in the ninth inning made another seventh game a necessity.

This was the American League's turn to host the tiebreaker, so the Twins' indoor horror site would decide the winner of this exciting World Series. The '91 Series had so far been one of the closest and most competitive World Series ever. Four of the previous games were decided by a run, and two went into extra innings.

Game Seven looked like another cliffhanger. Neither club wanted to be the first to blink. Both starters, Smoltz for the Braves, and Jack

Morris for the Twins, were on top of their games. Neither team could cross the plate, as the climax to a sterling World Series showdown raced inexorably toward the finish line. Each team had gotten a base runner to third base, but neither could advance a man another ninety feet.

Followers of the sport wondering when a seventh game had last produced such a double zip had to reach back in their memories to 1968. In that one, Tiger lefty Mickey Lolich hooked up with the great Bob Gibson of the Cardinals, producing six scoreless innings. Detroit finally broke through for three in the seventh inning on the way to a 4-1 victory, which brought them the title.

The eighth inning dawned, and it appeared as if the Braves might draw first blood. With runner Lonnie Smith on first base, Terry Pendleton ripped a Jack Morris serve to deep left-center field. Smith had gotten the green light, so he started to streak for second, hoping to steal the base. The ball rattled off the canvas barrier and bounced around like it had struck the edge of a pool table.

Smith could have crawled home on his hands and knees, but when the dust cleared, there stood Lonnie, glued to third base, looking more like a cigar store Indian than an Atlanta Brave. Smith had apparently lost the ball in the lights and quirky white ceiling and held up at third. Although the abhorrent conditions of the Metrodome appeared to be jinxing yet another visiting team, the Atlanta players in the dugout were all able to pick up the flight of the ball. Only Smith seemed lost in the whiteout.

Given this huge break, Morris bore down. He retired the next batter on a ground out and intentionally walked the dangerous David Justice to fill the sacks. The next hitter, lead-footed Sid Bream, validated the strategy as he rapped into a double play.

Double plays also helped the Braves out of jams in the eighth and ninth innings. In each frame, the Twins threatened to score. In the eighth, Minnesota loaded the bases with one out, but first-baseman Kent Hrbek's double-play grounder saved Atlanta from further damage.

In the ninth, with the Championship Trophy on the line, Chili Davis and Brian Harper opened with hits, but reliever Alejandro Pena induced Shane Mack into grounding into another double play. The twin-killing left a runner on third, so Braves' manager Bobby Cox ordered an intentional pass for Mike Pagliarulo. With a chance to be the World Series hero, pinch-hitter Paul Sorrento then struck out.

Never before in World Series history had a seventh game gone scoreless through the regulation nine innings. Twins' manager Tom Kelly surprised everyone by allowing Morris to go out to the mound for the tenth stanza. He warned his ace that it would be his last inning regardless of what happened.

Morris retired the side in order, and the Twins came to bat for the tenth time in this gem. Dan Gladden started the inning with a broken-bat hit into short left field that he legged into a double. Rookie-of-the-Year Chuck Knoblauch bunted Gladden to third.

With two all-star hitters, Puckett and Hrbek, due up, Pena was not taking any chances. He walked both men, since the Braves needed another double play. Furthermore, only the runner at third mattered anyway.

The pinch-batter was a reserve outfielder named Gene Larkin. Larkin had played sparingly all year, but while attending Columbia University, he had broken all of Lou Gehrig's hitting records.

Larkin waited patiently for the right pitch. He finally lashed it over the drawn-in outfield, for the Series-winning hit, and the Minnesota Twins were World Champs for the second time in four years.

The 1991 World Series was one of the most closely-contested and competitive of any that a pair of rivals ever played. Jack Morris won the Series MVP award for his two outstanding wins, which included this ten-inning masterpiece.

This was only the second Game Seven that went into extra innings and only the second time a seventh game ended 1 to 0. The only other time that happened was in the 1962 thriller, when the Yankees squeaked by the Giants by that score, with the potential winning runs stranded on second and third.

Except for the base running blunder, whereby Lonnie Smith could have scored the run that would have made extra innings unnecessary, the Braves didn't lose the World Series as much as the Twins won it. National League clubs that might have to face Minnesota in a future confrontation would be wise to make sure they won a pennant in an even-numbered year, when they would have the seventh game at home.

TWINS-BRAVES RECAP

	R	H	E
Minnesota	1	10	0
Atlanta	0	7	0

Winning pitcher- Morris
Losing pitcher- Pena
Home runs- none

HEROES ** Morris, Larkin
GOAT < L. Smith

1992

MAJOR HEADLINES

A violent civil riot sweeps Los Angeles after a jury acquits four white policemen charged with the vicious beating of motorist Rodney King. Some of the actual beating is caught on video tape, and the resulting riot kills fifty-two people and paralyzes the Los Angeles area for several days.

The United States leads a U.N.-sanctioned military force into Somalia.

Arkansas Governor Bill Clinton defeats President George Bush to win the 1992 presidential election.

Hurricane Andrew devastates parts of South Florida with property losses estimated at $15 to $20 million.

Serial killer Jeffrey Dahmer, who murdered and mutilated fifteen people, is given fifteen consecutive terms of life imprisonment.

Former Heavyweight boxing champion Mike Tyson receives a six-year prison sentence for rape.

SPORTS

Baseball: Toronto Blue Jays beat Atlanta in a six-game World Series.

Pro Football: Washington downs Buffalo in Super Bowl XXVI. ('91 Season)

College Football: Alabama wins the National Championship.

Pro Basketball: Chicago is repeat NBA champion by defeating Portland.

College Basketball: Duke repeats as NCAA champion by defeating Michigan in final.

Hockey: Pittsburgh wins second straight Stanley Cup title by beating Chicago in finals.

U.S. Open Tennis-
    Men's Finals: Stefan Edberg beats Pete Sampras.
    Women's Finals: Monica Seles beats Arantxa Sanchez-Vicario.

MOVIES- ACADEMY AWARDS

Best Actor: Al Pacino, *Scent of a Woman*
Best Actress: Emma Thompson, *Howard's Run*
Best Director: Clint Eastwood, *Unforgiven*
Best Picture: *Unforgiven*

CHAPTER XLIX
FRANCISCO WHO?

Wednesday, October 14, 1992- Fulton County Stadium, Atlanta, GA
National League Championship Series, Game Seven
Atlanta Braves 3, Pittsburgh Pirates 2

Who could ask for anything more? The seventh game of the playoff for the National League pennant going down to the last out in the bottom of the ninth, with the bases loaded and the home team trailing by a run—it doesn't get any better than that.

The Pittsburgh Pirates and Atlanta Braves created such a scenario in Game Seven of the 1992 National League Championship Series at Atlanta's Fulton County Stadium, the home of the Braves. Both teams were highly motivated to advance to the World Series, and the loser would suffer a painful defeat.

Pittsburgh had won three consecutive NL East titles, but the Pirates had suffered upset losses in the NLCS the past two years. The Braves, defending champions of the Senior Circuit, and the Cincinnati Reds, who won it all in 1990, knocked off the favored Bucs in each of the last two National League showdowns. The economics of the swiftly-changing national pastime indicted that small-market Pittsburgh would soon lose much of its team to the larger, more lucrative organizations. Free Agency was nothing more than extortion to small-market clubs like the Pirates, thus for them, the urgency to win was immediate.

The Braves enjoyed playing in the World Series in 1991 so much that they wanted to do it again. Since they suffered the heartbreaking tenth-inning loss in the final game of that spectacular classic, the Braves were missing only one ingredient to attain total satisfaction, a World Series victory. Since, as in the lottery, you can't win it if you're not in it, the Atlantans' first task was to turn back the Pirates so they could get another shot at the title.

After the Braves had soared to a three-games-to-one lead, Pittsburgh won the next two encounters and threatened to become the first National League team to rally from that deficit to capture the pennant. Momentum had switched to the Pirates, especially after their sixth-game 13 to 4 thrashing of the Braves, one of the worst drubbings Atlanta had suffered since General Sherman came to town.

In his zeal to win, Bucs' manager Jim Leyland had his ace right-hander, Doug Drabek, ready to start his third game of the series. John Smoltz, who was the hard-luck starter in the seventh game of the '91 World Series, was manager Bobby Cox' choice. Smoltz had already won two playoff games against Drabek, so this game matched the opposing hurlers for the third time.

In this second rematch, Drabek was getting the better of the battle. Pittsburgh scored in its first batting turn on a walk, an Andy VanSlyke double, and a sac fly. Drabek nursed the slim lead into the sixth, when Jay Bell doubled and VanSlyke singled in the second run.

The Pirates threatened to break open the game in the seventh and eighth innings, but like the Red Sox and Cubs before them, their bats could not produce the big hit that would insure their triumphal desires.

In the seventh, VanSlyke flied out to center stranding three base runners. In the eighth, Jeff King doubled, but when the runner at first, Orlando Merced, tried to score, right-fielder David Justice gunned him down with a perfect throw to the plate.

Meanwhile Drabek, pitching with tenacity and courage, had maintained a five-hit shutout entering the fateful ninth inning. He escaped a bases-loaded, no-out situation in the sixth stanza and worked out of another jam with two runners on and one out in the seventh. Entering the bottom of the ninth, the Pirates could taste their first pennant in thirteen years.

Terry Pendleton opened the Braves' ninth with a double into the right field corner. Then, gold-glove second-baseman Jose Lind bobbled an easy ground ball hit by Justice. Lind was one of the game's premier defensive players, but he just couldn't come up with the grounder this time.

When Drabek walked Sid Bream, his night had ended. Leyland summoned Stan Belinda from the bullpen, the Pirate leader in saves with eighteen. Ron Gant then backed Barry Bonds to the wall in left field, where he made the catch. The sacrifice fly drove in Atlanta's first run.

Belinda issued the second free pass of the inning to Damon Berryhill to reload the sacks. The reliever induced an infield pop up from Brian

Hunter for what would have been the pennant-winning third out if not for Lind's error.

This set the climactic confrontation of the National League season in motion. With the pitcher's spot due up, Cox called for third-string catcher Francisco Cabrera to dust the cobwebs off his seat on the bench and grab a bat. With the regular backstop Greg Olson out of action with a broken leg, Cabrera moved up on the depth chart.

Cabrera had one other at-bat in the Series and only ten plate appearances during the season, but this AB was to become the experience of his career. Cabrera smacked a 2-1 pitch between third and short for a hard single.

Justice scored the tying run, and Bream, a six-cylinder hitter but only a four-cylinder runner, chugged around the bases right behind him. Bonds fielded the ball and made a fine throw to the plate. Bream slid under the glove of catcher Mike LaVallier to barely beat the tag.

In one of baseball's most thrilling comebacks and dramatic finishes, the Braves had rallied for three runs in their last batting turn to defeat the Pirates for the second straight year. They were repeat champions of the National League.

The impact of this Kodak Moment caused distinctly different reactions. The Braves rejoiced in jubilation on the field, mobbing their new hero. The Pirate players, who had seen their dreams shattered within twenty-two brief pitches, also remained on the field, numb and disbelieving. They appeared too paralyzed to walk back to their clubhouse.

This was the second time that the Steel City club had lost a playoff series after leading the deciding game in the ninth inning. The '72 Pirates led Cincinnati by a run in the fifth game, only to see Johnny Bench homer to tie the contest and their pitcher, Bob Moose, wild-pitch the Reds to the flag.

For Atlanta, Francisco Cabrera briefly escaped a world of anonymity to earn his moment in the national spotlight. His name and picture would adorn newspapers and magazines all over the nation, and even earn a mention from President Bush during his re-election campaign.

Although he would eventually retreat back to his obscure world after the season ended, Francisco Cabrera could never forget this magic moment in his career, and one of the most dramatic moments in baseball history.

BRAVES-PIRATES RECAP

	R	H	E
Atlanta	3	7	0
Pittsburgh	2	7	1

Winning pitcher- Reardon
Losing pitcher- Drabak
Home runs- none

HEROES ** Justice, Cabrera
GOATS << Lind, Belinda

1993

MAJOR HEADLINES

A powerful bomb planted by international terrorists explodes in a World Trade Center parking garage in New York City killing six people and injuring more than 1000.

An unsuccessful raid on the Branch Dividian complex in Waco, TX kills four federal agents. When armored vehicles pump the compound with tear gas, cult members inside respond with gunfire and burn down the compound, leaving seventy dead.

Janet Reno is appointed the first woman Attorney General by President Clinton.

A major flood inundates nine Midwestern states, leaving fifty dead and property losses estimated at $12 billion.

A major gun control law known as the "Brady Bill" is signed into law by President Clinton.

SPORTS

Baseball: Toronto is repeat champion by beating Philadelphia in six games in the World Series.

Pro Football: Dallas thrashes Buffalo in Super Bowl XXVII. ('92 Season)

College Football: Florida State is voted the National Champion.

Pro Basketball: Chicago whips the Phoenix Suns for their third straight NBA title.

College Basketball: North Carolina defeats Michigan in the NCAA final.

Hockey: Montreal defeats Los Angeles in the Stanley Cup finals.

U.S. Open Tennis-
    Men's Finals: Pete Sampras beats Cedric Pioline.
    Women's Finals: Steffi Graff defeats Helena Sukova.

MOVIES- ACADEMY AWAR

Best Actor: Tom Hanks, *Philadelphia*
Best Actress: Holly Hunter, *The Piano*
Best Director: Steven Spielberg, *Schindler's List*
Best Picture: *Schindler's List*

CHAPTER L
MIGHTY JOE CARTER

Saturday, October 23, 1993- Skydome, Toronto, ON, CAN
World Series Game Six, Toronto Blue Jays 8, Philadelphia Phillies 6

In 1992, a baseball milestone had been achieved. When the Toronto Blue Jays won the American League pennant, the World Series would stage games outside the United States for the first time in history. Then, when the Blue Jays won the Series, they became the first team to ever bring a World Championship title to Canada.

Now Toronto looked to repeat, as they led the National League champion Philadelphia Phillies by a three-games-to-two margin. As Game Six of the 1993 World Series was about to start at the Skydome in the beautiful Canadian city, the Jays needed only one more victory to retain the crown.

The Phillies had surprised everyone by surviving the NL Championship Series against Atlanta, but the Braves seemed to run out of gas after their grueling pennant chase of the Giants. The Braves had overcome a huge San Francisco lead to win the Western Division title on the final day of the season, while the Phils had an easier time capturing the East flag.

No club likes to be dependent on a seventh game when t hey can put it away in six. The heavy-hitting Blue Jays started in this manner. After five innings, they had socked Philadelphia pitching for five runs and led 5 to 1.

Paul Molitor, the omnipotent Toronto designated hitter, always seemed to figure in every Jay scoring drive during this October final. Molitor tripled in a run in the first inning and eventually scored on a sac fly, as the Canadians scored three times in their first batting turn. In the fifth, with the score at 4-1, he smacked a homer to give Toronto a seemingly safe four-run cushion.

Rather than meekly capitulate, the stubborn Phillie team rallied in a big five-run seventh to make the seventh-inning stretch a nervous one for the Blue Jay fans. The Phillie sparkplug was their brilliant centerfielder, former Met Lennie Dykstra. Dykstra came to the Phils in a blockbuster trade, which was one of the worst deals in New York since the Indians traded Manhattan Island to the Dutch for some costume jewelry.

Dykstra's three-run home run started the Philadelphia comeback and knocked out the Toronto starter, Dave Stewart, the former Oakland stalwart. The circuit clout was Dykstra's fourth in this World Series. In this Series, Lenny was like a one-man army, doing his best to prevent the Blue Jays from repeating as champs.

After Dykstra's home run, the Quakers added another two markers on a base on balls and three more hits. Thus they held a 6-5 lead, which they carried into the home half of the ninth frame. Another dramatic ninth inning, like so many in previous playoff and World Series contests, was about to take place.

The Phils' closer, Mitch Williams (a.k.a. Wild Thing) got the call to make sure there would be a seventh game. In the incredulous fourth game, Williams entered the contest to protect a ninth-inning 14-10 lead and surrendered five runs. The 15-14 loss made it appear as if Toronto went for the two-point conversion and made it.

Now Williams issued a lead-off walk to speedster Rickey Henderson. Normally this is akin to giving up a double. However, with feared hitters like Molitor and Joe Carter waiting on the bench, Rickey stayed close to first base.

Molitor, as was becoming the custom, lashed a one-out single to put the tying and winning runs on base, the tying one in scoring position. Then up to the plate stepped Carter.

The Jays' right-fielder was one of the most popular players in Canada. Before the start of the season, Carter declined Free Agency and signed a contract extension to remain in Toronto.

His teammates and fans were glad that he was staying, but never as thrilled as the next moment, when he drilled a 2-2 delivery from the ill-fated Williams deep into the left field seats for the crusher that brought the Toronto Blue Jays an 8 to 6 victory and their second consecutive World Championship.

The victorious players hoisted their hero into the air and remained on the field to continue their celebration. Since crowd control is not as serious a problem in Toronto as it is in most American cities, many of the fans joined in on the carpet. No one wanted to leave the ballpark on this gala night of exaltation.

The Carter home run marked the sixth time that a World Series ended without a final out. On five other occasions, a hit by the final batter decided the outcome, most recently in 1991. In that Fall Classic, Gene Larkin's tenth-inning hit broke a scoreless tie in the seventh game and gave the Twins a 1 to 0 decision over the Braves. In 1926 Babe Ruth tried unsuccessfully to steal a base, instead becoming the final out of the Series.

The only other time a World Series ended with a home run occurred in 1960, when Pirate second-baseman Bill Mazeroski struck the fatal blow that defeated the Yankees in a singular seventh game. Carter thus joined some mighty select company with his dynamic circuit breaker.

The Toronto Blue Jays became the first team since the Yankees of 1977 and '78 to win back-to-back World Championships. Winning the World Series is hard enough, but repeating has become monumental if you're not the Yankees.

Paul Molitor may have been the Series MVP, but it's Mighty Joe Carter whom Toronto fans will always remember for the joy and pride he spread throughout that city and all of Canada. With one swing of his bat, he brought the Blue Jays from behind to a sudden-death victory. Future World Series will find it hard to duplicate the thrill and the drama of that moment.

BLUE JAYS-PHILLIES RECAP

	R	H	E
Toronto	8	10	2
Philadelphia	6	7	0

Winning pitcher- Ward
Losing pitcher- M. Williams
Home runs- Molitor, Dykstra, Carter

HEROES ** Molitor, Carter
GOAT < M. Williams

ACKNOWLEDGEMENTS

Chronicle of America

Chronicle of the 20th Century

World Almanac and Book of Facts

The Series-an Illustrated History of Baseball's Postseason Showcase

The New York Times

The New York Post

The New York Daily News

The Newark Star-Ledger

The Yogi Book

ESPN Classic Sports Network

Baseball Hall of Fame and Museum

WCBS-TV Channel 2

WNBC-TV Channel 4

The Birds

Network

Rocky

Titanic

Former President Jimmy Carter

Al Jolson

Edgar Allan Poe

ABOUT THE AUTHOR

Warren Goldfein is attempting to fulfill a lifelong dream by publishing his first book. Goldfein has always had a love for the printed word. He actively wrote for the college literary magazine and was a sports reporter for the college newspaper at Muhlenberg College, where he graduated with a degree in English.

Since his college days, Goldfein has submitted articles to newspapers and magazines, many of which are related to current topics of the day. He usually laces his writings with humor and sarcasm. "There is enough tragedy in everything we read in the newspapers, hear on the radio, or see on TV, so when I write, I'd rather entertain the reader and make him laugh a little," he explains.

With all his writings, Goldfein has never put together that full-length book he has always wanted to do - until now. He is 69 years old, married, with two children and two grand children. He lives in Northern New Jersey and still works every day as an auto insurance underwriter. "As long as I remain in good health, There is no reason for me not to keep working," he says. While he maintains his career is business, he now intends to continue his other career as a writer.

CPSIA information can be obtained
at www.ICGtesting.com
Printed in the USA
FSOW02n1413110917
38521FS